KATIE SAOIDHBH MCGREAL

YOU WERE NEVER THE
PROBLEM
STORIES TO CONFIRM IT IS NOT YOUR FAULT

Copyright © 2024
You are not the Problem
By
Katie Saoidhbh McGreal

All rights are reserved

No part of this book may be used or reproduced in any manner without written permission from the author, except in the case of brief quotations used in articles or reviews.

For information contact Katie

All names in these stories have been changed for privacy reasons.

CREDITS

Cover designer: Wingfield Designs
Editor: Caroline Stainburn @Wizard editing
Formatter: V.R Formatting

For Amy, who taught me that I didn't need to do anything to be loved

TRIGGER WARNING

This book contains mentions of parental abuse, neglect, bullying and there is mention of sexual harassment

FOREWORD.

I can barely believe that you are reading this because that means I have written and published it! My intention with this book is to offer insight into parental abuse. I want to provide sufferers and survivors support and validation, and I want to shed some light on what parental abuse is. I hope you find it informative, insightful and inspiring. The stories were challenging to write, but I hope they are educational and entertaining.

All the stories are based loosely, some not so loosely, around different things that happened in the household and family unit I grew up in during the 90s in Dublin. All names are changed to protect privacy.

My home was not a safe place for me growing up. I didn't know it wasn't safe, but I do now. No one talked about parental abuse in the 90s. We were starting to learn about sexual abuse during those years. It was in the news. I remember being told about the man who raped a schoolgirl near where I went to school. I was told not to walk

FOREWORD

places alone at night. I knew that there were bad men out there who raped women. But I wasn't sexually abused, so there was nothing wrong, right? When it came to people's families and home lives, we were actively encouraged to not get involved and to not ask questions. This meant anything uncomfortable happening within the home was not spoken about or acknowledged.

Biologically, we are hardwired to cling to our parents. We need them to survive. They feed us, clothe us, house us. Our brain tells us that, without our parents, we will not survive, so no matter how they treat us or what happens, we will stick to them. For a lot of parental abuse survivors, we have even spent years protecting our parents. We stand up for them, we offer them help and even money sometimes. We will do anything for our parents because, biologically, we need them to survive.

So, if you, as an adult like me, realised that your parents weren't okay. If you realise what they did and said to you was wrong, forgive yourself for protecting them. Forgive yourself for staying in a situation that was unsafe because you were following your biology. As adults, we can choose to leave difficult situations. We do not have that choice or option as children.

Parental abuse can and does take many forms. My experience was emotional and mental abuse, which included a lot of bullying from both parents and siblings. I was not shown any love as a child. I was ridiculed for crying and even for liking the things that I liked, but I have learnt in recent years that this was not normal behaviour and it was not everyone's experience. I have also learnt that I was not the problem. The family dynamic I was raised in made me believe I was the problem. I caused all of the issues, and if I could be better, be quieter, and be more like them, everything would be better, but I was never the problem. It was never my responsibility to fix anything or to change. My parents were supposed to protect me, not the other way around.

For anyone who resonates with my words and who resonates with these stories, I am sending you so much love. There is a list of charities and organisations that may be able to offer you support at the back of this book. I have also included a podcast I have loved and a book suggestion so you can learn more. I hope they help. Please know you are not alone, you are not broken, and it was not your fault. You did nothing wrong. You are perfect and loveable, just as you are. They were the problem. Not you.

She's Forgotten Me

Jess stared at her phone. She'd been staring at it for two days, and she hadn't gotten so much as an email.

She's forgotten about me, Jess thought; she's forgotten about me again. She can't even remember me when we're in the middle of a fight!

Two days ago, Jess had gotten a text from her Mum;

> Mum: It's so disappointing that we're not going to see you over the weekend.
> Christina is very disappointed.

> Jess: I told you, I have plans already and I have things I need to do here.

> Mum: Could you not do them at home?
> She's very disappointed.

Jess gritted her teeth. She still hadn't heard from Christina. 'She can't be that disappointed if she can't even contact me herself!' Jess thought furiously, 'She never even asked me herself to come home for God's sake!'

> Jess: No, I have to be here to get them done. Christina could always come and visit me sometime.

> Mum: But this is a bit different. You could make the effort for her birthday.

'Like she's made such an effort before, for my birthday,' Jess fumed, thinking about all of the times she'd to go to them on her birthday.

> Jess: You could both come down next weekend. Make it another celebration of Christina's birthday.

> Mum: I can't do it next weekend. Emily might need me. She's got the baby.

Jess rolled her eyes. She'd expected that. Her mum had spent at least six months now saying she should really come and visit her but she never actually did. She had expected an excuse, but it still hurt .

> Jess: Is her husband not there to help her?

> Mum: I'd just like to be available in case they need me.

> Jess: But what about me needing you? You hardly ever come to see me!

Jess could feel the tears welling up now. The frustration, anger and unfairness of Jess always being told to go home but no one ever wanting to come and see her, all becoming too much

> Mum: That's not true. I came down and we went to that lovely restaurant.

> Jess: When Dad was working in Castlebar, and you stayed for two hours and then had to leave?

Jess was fuming. How could she think that coming over for a few hours was enough? Here her mum was, demanding that she drop everything at the last minute to celebrate her sister's birthday - a birthday the birthday girl had told her to not come home for - and yet with a week's notice, her mum still couldn't find the time to come and see Jess herself.

> Mum: Don't be like that, Jessica. I don't know what's gotten into you. I have visited you plenty of times. There's no need for you to play the 'poor me' card. You're making Christina's birthday all about you by being so stubborn.

> Jess: I was at home two weeks ago. Christina told me she wasn't going to be there for her birthday so not to come back and you haven't visited me for more than a few hours ever, but yet I have to drop everything at the last minute so as to not upset Christina!

And now, two days later, Jess was still waiting for a reply.

Jess used to go home every other weekend without fail.

She'd be there for every birthday, public holiday, basically whenever they asked. Jess was at home all the time, despite the fact that she hadn't lived there in over nine years. She didn't live there intentionally. She didn't like Dublin; didn't like the sprawling-ness of it or how busy and big it felt. She had no interest in living in a city anymore, a fact she knew was something her parents could not resonate with.

Their last two-hour visit had come on the day she was going to look at her first property to rent outside Galway city. The phone rang as Jess was washing her breakfast dishes. "We're just driving from Castlebar now," Mum had announced, "Are you free to meet us in about an hour, an hour and a half?"

As usual, this was the first Jess had heard about their visit. She hadn't had any warning they would possibly be dropping by. She used to think that the beauty of living so far away was that they would never drop in completely unannounced, as they did to her sister Emily, but that had apparently not been the case. Jess would have plans, but they were usually dropped when she got a call like that. She was just so excited to have her parents visit her, and have them show interest in her for once. However, this time, she couldn't just drop her plans, and she didn't want to, either. Jess was desperately looking for somewhere new to rent before her current landlord evicted her, and despite not wanting to tell her parents that she was looking to move out of the city, she had never been able to lie to her mum. It felt like a physical impossibility not to tell her everything, so she found herself blurting out.

"I have a house viewing at one, so I'll have to meet you after."

"Oh, very good! Where is it?"

"In Indreabhán,"

"Indreabhán? Where's that?"

"Out in Conamara; outside the city,"

"Oh right," Jess could picture her mother's shocked and disapproving face, "So you're looking to live in the country?"

"Yes,"

Jess had wanted to leave the city for years, but she hadn't known how, or so she thought. In truth, she knew her parents would disapprove, and they'd tell her it would be so difficult for a single woman out in the country where everyone already knew each other, and wouldn't Jess get lonely? She couldn't face the repercussions that she knew would come if she did what she wanted to do.

"Well, that'll be different."

"When is the viewing?" Jess's Dad suddenly said, and Jess realised she must be on speakerphone.

"In an hour and a half."

"Well why don't we meet you there?" he said.

Jess clenched her fist and took a slow breath. "No," she finally replied.

"Why not?"

"Because I don't want you to come." Her teeth were clenched now. She wanted to go on her own. They had never been interested in house viewings before. 'Why did I say anything? I should have just lied', she berated herself.

"But I could pretend that it's me looking to rent it," Dad said.

"And what difference would that make?"

"You never know, you might get a better deal."

"No. I will meet you afterwards."

"Suit yourself," Dad said.

"So, you'll call us when you're finished there then?" Mum was back.

"Yes. I'll call you."

'Now they're angry with me', she thought to herself, staring at her phone miserably. 'Why did I say anything?' She wondered again. 'Why can't I keep my big mouth shut?'

By the time Jess met her parents in An Spidéal after the viewing, they'd had time to digest the information, and neither of them said much about it. But Jess knew she would hear from her sister, Emily, in a few days, and she would tell her what they really thought.

Emily was the oldest of the three girls. Jess was the middle child and Christina was the youngest, and was still treated and acted like the baby. Jess knew her mother would call Emily on the way back to Dublin, she could almost imagine the conversation.

"She's looking to move out to the country," Mum would say.

"Oh, on her own?" Emily would reply with surprise.

"Yes, and she'll be living on her own as well. I don't know why she seems to want to isolate herself so much. She's always been so independent," Mum would continue in a judging tone.

"I know, I don't understand it either. If she could just find someone nice to settle down with, she would be much happier," Emily would join in.

"She just can't seem to keep a man. I don't know what's wrong with her. If she would meet someone and settle down like you, she would be so much happier. They could buy a house and she wouldn't have to be moving all the time. She finds the moving so stressful."

"But she doesn't do anything to help herself. She could even look into getting a mortgage herself and buy somewhere. Then at least there would be no more pressure to move."

"And you know we would help her out with that but she just doesn't want that. She's just so stubborn and bull-headed."

Jess knew how the conversation would go because Emily always relayed them to her. She always found out what her mother really thought of her decisions and life choices from her sister. No matter how much Jess didn't think she really needed to know. Emily had come to her, telling her how much their mother had hated her tattoo a few years previously. Jess was sitting at the kitchen table when Emily had come in and told her.

"She said 'I don't know why she even showed me! I hate tattoos and she knows that'," Emily said, sitting across from her sister.

"Oh!" Jess looked down at the little heart on her wrist in surprise, "I didn't know she hated them," she finally said.

"Apparently she's said it in the past sometime," Emily shrugged. "Oh well! Who cares?"

Jess sat back in her seat feeling dejected. She had shown her mum because she had asked what Jess had been up to that week. She hadn't realised that her mother hated it. Mum hadn't really said much, but Jess didn't take that as a sign of her hating it.

A few days after the visit from her parents, and after finally securing a new home to live in outside the city, Jess got a text from Emily.

> Emily: Mum says you're moving out of the city. She's worried that you'll be lonely living out there all by yourself.

Jess rolled her eyes. That was what she had been expecting.

Moving out of the city was one of the best decisions

Jess had ever made. She loved the quiet and the fields around her, and her neighbours were great. They fixed things in the flat when it was needed and one of them even changed the tyre on her car when he had noticed it was flat. Her landlady was so kind, and every month when she went in to pay rent, they had tea and a chat. It was the first time in years that Jess had lived alone, and she absolutely loved it. She loved being able to do whatever she wanted, whenever she wanted, with no consequences for anyone else. So, despite her mother's insistence that she would be lonely and wouldn't last long out there, or would want to move back to the city soon, Jess had thrived.

For years, Jess had been sharing houses with strangers; some were lovely and kind, and she had gotten on so well with them, but some she had not. There had been different atmospheres in each of the houses, and they weren't all nice, but living alone, Jess created her own atmosphere. She created how she wanted the house to feel and be, and it felt empowering.

Loving the home she had designed for herself, meant that Jess didn't want to leave it but she still felt the obligation from her parents to visit all the time. She decided one Saturday evening, when everyone was sitting down to dinner, she had to tell them.

"I won't be coming back to Dublin as much as I am anymore," she blurted out, "I'm exhausted and all of the travelling up and down to Dublin isn't sustainable."

Her mum looked at her in surprise.

"I'm so tired I can barely stand. I'll come back once a month from now on, and I'll only be back for big birthdays and Christmas, that's it. I can't keep going like I am right now."

"Hmm," Mum said, and no one else spoke.

That night, Jess lay in her childhood bed staring at the ceiling. Sleep never came easily to her in her parent's house. She spent many nights lying awake, waiting to doze off but it usually took hours. Her mind was a constant hive of activity and it seemed to be worse when she was in her old bedroom. She wished she could visit for an evening and then leave again. She wished visiting didn't require the whole weekend.

After that, Jess decided that she had set her parents up for her not visiting as often. She had said it outright, and there had been no objections or even comments, so now, they should expect her at the house less.

Three months in and Jess had stuck to her commitment to go back once a month and she was happy with it. She felt so much better and in control of her own time and her mother seemed to be appeased, so that box was checked. But, now that she wasn't around her family as much, the tense and stressful atmosphere in her parent's home, when she was there, was impossible to ignore.

Her sister, Christina, was still living at home, and was one of the most negative people Jess had ever met. There was always something for her to complain about. Work was the most common, but then she also complained about the neighbours making too much noise, or the men she went on dates with not being attentive enough, or not listening to her. When Jess lived at home, she'd barely noticed Christina's negativity; in fact, she and Emily had enjoyed complaining about Christina, but now that Jess was spending less time there, when she was around, she found it draining. And Christina was clearly missing having her sister available to her all the time.

"You're never here!" she moaned one Sunday after Jess

told her that she couldn't go to a comedy gig with her the following Saturday.

"I've been here all weekend!"

Jess looked over to where her mother was sitting, reading the paper. She hoped her mum might jump in and defend her, because how could she possibly be at home more than she currently was, without actually just moving home?

"But now you're leaving again. You're always leaving! You're not here enough! I just want to spend time with you." Jess thought Christina looked like she was going to cry and the guilt almost crippled her.

"But I don't live here," Jess said, "I have to go." but even she could feel the lameness of the words. She, of course, didn't have to go. She could stay. She knew she could stay. But she didn't want to.

She couldn't get Christina's words out of her head as she sat on the bus back to Galway later that day.

'Maybe I should be at home more,' she thought to herself, 'maybe I should go to that thing with her next weekend. Ugh, I hate this! Why can't I just live…wait a minute;' her logical brain kicked in the further she got from her parent's house. 'I was there all weekend and Christina was out with friends, and then on some date! I was there and she didn't bother actually spending time with me because it didn't suit her! And I was there last weekend. I don't live there, I have a life!'

The anger was real. It was strong and unforgiving. And it was all directed at Christina.

'How dare she make out I don't do enough,' Jess raged inside her own head, 'she has visited me once since I moved to Galway, four years ago, and she's complaining that I don't go home enough? The audacity!'

The woman sitting beside Jess on the bus looked at her with concern. Jess realised that she must have been glaring at her. She smiled quickly and averted her eyes to look out the window.

After this realisation on the Citylink bus, everything started to unravel. Jess was thinking more and more about her relationship with her different family members. The more she thought about it, the less she wanted to go home, and the more she was starting to come into her own. Doing what she loved and what made her happy. Jess had always loved hiking but could never seem to find the time for it, so she found a local group that went out on Sundays, and started hiking with them. But that meant that she had to be in Galway on Sunday so she couldn't go home. She had an excuse now, a reason to not go home.

The less Jess was at home the more she started to realise that her mum was calling a lot less. She used to call at least once a week, and always during the day when Jess was trying to work, and the conversations would last for hours. She would still get a text on Friday asking what she was doing for the weekend, but no call; no one contacting her to see how she was.

The realisation that her siblings barely ever contacted her to see how she was, was hurtful. Jess would get the odd text from Emily, if Mum had been talking about her and Emily felt the need to report back, but nothing else. Jess talked to Christina when she was actually in her parent's house, but Christina never called or texted just to see how she was. Dad never called either, not unless he wanted something, whether that was Jess to do work for him or he was requesting that she stop being mean to Christina and to just do what she was asking, whatever that was at the time.

Mum's Friday texts were the only regular occurrence, the one thing she had that connected her to Dublin, to her family. As time went on, Jess started to realise the only time her mum called her now was when she put something into the family WhatsApp group. Jess would occasionally message what she was doing at the weekend, or would ask a question about Ryanair's new baggage rules, and then she would get a call almost immediately.

"She's forgotten me. She's forgotten her middle daughter. She needs to physically see me in her house for her to remember I exist," Jess confided to her best friend, Ann. "And then I wonder if I'm crazy, and imagining all of these things, but I can't be because it just keeps happening!"

As the months went on, Jess had felt her relationship with her mother was becoming more strained. It was more difficult to ignore how little interest she seemed to have in her. Jess was aware of feeling uncomfortable, feeling forgotten, and left out of the family, but was afraid to mention anything. She was having fewer actual conversations with her mother, but yet when the conversations did occur, they felt like the warm conversations Jess remembered, so she didn't want to rock the boat by questioning anything.

But Christina's birthday had felt like the last straw.

"I probably won't be here anyway," Christina had told Jess when she was in Dublin a few weeks before her actual birthday, "A few of us are planning a weekend in Kilkenny, and it'll be that weekend I think."

"Great. That'll be lovely to get away and you can celebrate your birthday too." Jess was delighted. If Christina wasn't going to be there she wouldn't need to feel guilty for not being there either.

Two days before the weekend of Christina's birthday, Jess got a call from her dad.

"Christina is very upset that you won't be here for her birthday," Dad said after asking after Jess's work.

Jess's mouth fell open with shock. "What?" she finally said, "But she won't be there. She told me she was going away."

"That hasn't worked out and she's very disappointed that you won't be here."

"But she didn't ask me to be there." Jess was really confused. She didn't know how her sister could be disappointed that she wasn't going to something she didn't know about.

"But you knew it was her birthday," Dad continued.

"But she wasn't going to be there because she was going away."

"And now she'll be at home, and she is very disappointed that you won't be here for the weekend." Jess sat back in her chair and said nothing. The phone was still held to her ear. She was being summoned home for an event she had been told wasn't going to happen, and apparently, she had even upset her sister. She was confused and knew that nothing was going to help her argument. She had no argument. She didn't even know what she was arguing about. She hadn't known Christina would be there, so how was it possible for her sister to be upset at her. "So will you be down then?" Dad asked after neither of them had spoken for a while.

"I've made plans."

"But it's Christina's birthday and she's very disappointed that you won't be coming down for it." The conversation was going nowhere. Jess hung up a few minutes later after listening again to how disappointed and upset Christina was.

She stared at her phone. What was she to do? She wanted to go hiking, and she was going to meet Ann for lunch on Saturday. She didn't want to go home but maybe she should. She didn't know what to do.

"Christina said that she wouldn't be there for her birthday and after confirming that, you made plans and now, with two day's notice, your dad is on the phone telling you, you have to go home and Christina is upset that you won't be there. But she never asked you to be there in the first place?" Ann was trying to make sense of what Jess had just told her. "So, you're calling me to tell me you're going to cancel on me because you're going home for the weekend?"

"Yes," Jess answered, wracked with guilt as she said it.

"Okay," Ann finally said, "But-" she paused again, not wanting to upset her friend. Ann knew that she was feeling conflicted and she didn't want to add to the confusion.

"But what?" Jess prompted her.

"Christina herself hasn't even called you. She hasn't contacted you at all. If it was really that big a deal to her, do you not think she should. Or she would? And two days before the weekend is a bit rich to expect you to just drop everything. It's a bit ridiculous," Ann paused again, "You do see that, right?"

Jess paused. "I know. It is crazy. I thought it was, but I wasn't fully sure."

"Do you want to go home this weekend?" Ann asked.

"No," Jess replied without hesitation.

"Then I'll see you on Saturday," her friend said and hung up.

Jess: Hey Christina, sorry I won't be there for your birthday this weekend. I didn't think you would be there so I made other plans, but I'll see you again in a few weeks. Have a great weekend.

Taking a deep breath Jess pressed send. It was read in a few minutes and she got no response. Then the phone buzzed. It was Mum.

"So, you won't be here to celebrate your baby sister's birthday?" Mum said when Jess finally found her courage and answered the phone. Mum didn't sound angry, she sounded disappointed, and that was so much worse.

"I already have plans," Jess said quietly, "And she told me she wouldn't be there."

"But it's her birthday."

"I know," Jess was regretting answering the phone. She was already feeling guilty and she didn't need her mother to reinforce it.

"Could you not change the plans?"

Jess didn't say anything. "I don't want to," she finally replied, "I wasn't planning on going home, and now I just don't want to."

"You don't want to celebrate your sister's birthday? That's not very nice, is it?" Again, Jess didn't say anything. "How would you like it if we didn't celebrate your birthday?" Mum continued. Jess sat with her guilt, feeling like a spoilt little child being told off for not doing the right thing.

"Well," Jess finally said, breaking the silence, "Christina didn't come to me for my birthday. I had to go to Dublin. None of you came here."

"Don't be like that," Mum said, "Making it all about you. This is Christina's birthday, not yours."

"But you just said how mean it was that I wasn't going

to celebrate her birthday and actually, she's never been here to celebrate mine."

"You're always here. We always do something for you here. That's what we've always done and you've never complained about it before. You're trying to make this all about you." There was a pause. "Well, I just wanted to call and say that we'd miss you."

And that was the end of that call. Jess was wracked with guilt. What was she going to do? She called Ann again.

"You don't want to go. Don't go," Ann reminded her, "You'll see her in a few weeks."

And now, two days later, on Saturday morning Jess sat at the kitchen counter staring at her phone.

Jess: *I was at home two weeks ago. Christina told me she wasn't going to be there for her birthday so not to come back, and you haven't visited me for more than a few hours ever, but yet I have to drop everything at the last minute so as to not upset Christina!*

This was the last message that had been sent. For two days Jess had been waiting for a reply. She had been waiting for her mother to continue the conversation but she was still waiting. She had been forgotten again.

The tension, stress, frustration and sadness were beginning to rise in her body. Her vision blurred as the tears came. Her mother had forgotten her again. She couldn't believe it, but then nothing had changed. She'd been forgotten for most of her life. This wasn't really anything new, but it felt different.

The tears were coming faster now, and she could feel it in her chest and stomach. Her whole body started to heave as she was racked with sadness and frustration. But for once, Jess just gave into it. She let it all out. Jess let herself cry until she felt like she had nothing left to give.

And then she sat still. Jess sat and let a beautiful feeling of euphoria, calm, and ease wash over her.

I don't have a family anymore, she thought. I don't have a family anymore, and it feels like the best thing ever.

Her phone buzzed. It was her mum.

Kissing

"So, are you and John dating now?" I was in the back garden, sitting under the tree with a book. Emily had just come out.

I looked up at her and shrugged, "I guess so."

"Have you kissed?" I shook my head and went back to my book.

"Do you want to?"

"I don't know." I really wanted my sister to go away because Janet had just found an unusual set of footprints in the snow, and it looked like they were going to lead the Secret Seven to the real thief.

"Is he coming over?"

"Emily, leave me alone, I'm reading." I didn't take my eyes from the page, and I gritted my teeth in an effort to get her to see how serious I was.

"I was just asking about your boyfriend," Emily said grumpily, and walked off.

John lived in a house that backed onto the same lane as ours. He, and his brother Michael, had been coming over to the back garden to play after school for a few months. Tilly and Sarah lived in another estate that backed onto our house, too, and had also been coming over to play. They didn't go to the same school as us, but we had met them when we were playing in the local park. It had been really fun having them all over most evenings. Christina usually wanted to play too, but when we could, we did our best to get away from her. She was too young to play with us.

I had always thought John was the nicest of everyone. His brother Michael was much older than us; he was Sarah's age, thirteen. But John was only ten, the same age as Emily and two years older than me. Even though he was the same age as Emily, he liked me more. He'd told me that the day before, when he'd asked if I wanted to go out with him.

My face lit up when he asked. No one liked me more than Emily, she was always more popular and outgoing. I said yes immediately, although I didn't know what it meant to go out with someone, but if it meant I got to spend more time with John, then I was happy with that.

"Hi Jess!" I looked up as Tilly jumped down from our back wall. Her sister, Sarah, followed quickly behind her.

"Are we going to start making the treehouse today?" Sarah asked.

"Yes!" I marked the page in my book and stood up, "Dad found planks of wood that we can nail together, and then we can put it up in the tree." I said as John and Michael walked through our back gate.

"Hi," I said, smiling at them. "Can you help us get the wood from the side of the house? We're going to make the base of the treehouse today." I was really excited to get started. We had been talking about this for weeks now. We wanted a proper den that we could hang out in.

As they gathered the wood under the tree, I found a hammer and nails, and Emily joined us. The boys started lining the wood up beside each other so we could nail it together.

"So have you two kissed yet?" Emily asked while I held a piece of wood in place as John held the nail on top of it, ready to hammer it in.

"Who?" Michael asked.

"Jess and John," said Emily. She was looking at me slyly. My stomach lurched. I knew she wasn't going to let this go.

"We're making the treehouse," I said, turning back to the wood I was holding.

"So, you haven't kissed?" Michael was smiling now.

"No," John replied.

"So why don't you do it now?" Michael's smile had changed to a smirk. He was standing beside Emily and his arms were crossed across his chest. They weren't going to let it go.

I looked at John, who looked back at me, and shrugged. I wanted to keep making the treehouse. John stood up, and I could tell from his face that he was uncomfortable. He stuffed his hands deep into his trouser pockets and shuffled his feet. I didn't know what else to do so I dropped the wood I was still holding and stood up slowly. John's gaze was on the ground, away from me. Sarah, Tilly, Emily and Michael were all watching us, and I was nervous. I turned towards John, and he finally looked at me. I wasn't sure what to do next. I could tell that John didn't know either, but he took a step closer to me. We leaned in, and I felt his lips on mine. They were soft.

"Ew! That's so gross," Christina said. I hadn't known she was there and I pulled away quickly. My face was hot with embarrassment and I stared down at the ground. My heart was pounding and my palms were sweating.

Christina was a tattle-tale, she was going to tell mum, and I was going to be in so much trouble. 'Please just let us make the treehouse,' I thought desperately. When I glanced at John he was staring at the ground and shuffling his feet in the dirt.

"Can we get on with making the treehouse now?" I finally said. My face was still hot with embarrassment and shame, but I hoped no one noticed. Michael, Sarah and Emily were laughing and Tilly looked uncomfortable.

"What were you doing?" Christina asked.

"They were kissing. That's what boyfriends and girlfriends do," Emily said, smirking at me. I could have kicked her.

"I didn't know you had a boyfriend," Christina looked at me and my face went a deeper shade of red. Christina always tells Mum everything, there was no way she was not going to tell her this, and when she told her, I was going to be in so much trouble. When I was four, Mum had caught me behind the couch with her friend's son, Richard. I don't remember what we were doing. I actually don't remember being behind the couch at all, but Mum still talks about it now. We must have been doing something awful and I knew that kissing John fell into that awful category. My stomach was in knots with anxiety.

"Can we just make the treehouse now?" I finally said, looking desperately from Michael and Emily to Tilly and Sarah, hoping that someone would help end the misery.

"Are you going to kiss again?" Christina asked.

"No," I said firmly, wishing Christina would just go away. John hadn't said anything. I wanted him to tell them to leave us alone, but he was still staring at the ground, and his face was a beetroot red colour.

We finally went back to the treehouse.

The next day, after much discussion we decided that the treehouse wasn't going to work. We didn't have the skills to make it sturdy enough for us to be able to use it as a house and actually stand on it. We abandoned the idea altogether.

"Why don't we make a fort?" Sarah suggested, "We could make it over by that wall," she pointed over to where the shrubs were. "There would be enough shelter from the bushes, as well."

The boys hadn't turned up, so Emily, Sarah, Tilly and I got plastic sheets that had been stored in the shed, and we tied them over the bushes so we had a half-enclosed fort underneath. We used an extra plastic sheet for the floor so we could sit inside without getting dirty. We brought out pillows and cushions to sit on, and Sarah decided she wanted to plait Emily's hair into two strands that came together at the bottom. John and Michael arrived on their bikes as I was carrying a chair out so Emily could sit on it and have her hair done. "What are you doing?" Michael asked when he saw me.

"I'm bringing out a chair for the fort," I replied, putting it down just outside the fort.

"No boys allowed," Tilly announced from inside.

I looked at her with surprise as she came out to take the chair from me, and brought it inside. "Why not?" John asked as Emily sat down and Sarah started brushing her hair.

"Because boys are stupid," Sarah said without looking up from her task.

"What?" I couldn't believe what I was hearing. When did boys become stupid?

"Well, we don't care anyway!" Michael said, throwing his leg over his bike and making as if to cycle away. "Do we John?" He looked at his brother, who was still standing beside his own bike.

"No, we don't want to go in anyway!" John replied, but he didn't make to leave.

"So, what's it going to be, Jess?" Sarah asked, "Are you going to be in here with us, or out there with them?"

I looked from one to the other. I couldn't decide. I liked them all. John was really nice and Michael was fun to be with, but I wanted Sarah to do my hair like that, too. It looked nice and I wanted to be like the older girls. I looked from the boys, back to the fort, and then back to the boys again. John shrugged when I hesitated, and started to follow his brother, who had already left on his bike. I went into the fort, but I felt awful about my decision.

The next day I went out to the lane that all of our house's backed onto. John was dribbling a football around his garden. He gave me a small smile when he saw me and came up to the fence.

"Yesterday sucked," he said, digging his hands deep into his pocket. His eyes were focused on a stone on the ground.

I nodded, looking at my own feet. "It did," I finally said, "I don't know why we suddenly hated boys."

"Michael kissed Sarah, and she now hates him." John informed me, looking at me now. He looked confused but relieved to be able to tell me.

"Oh!" My eight-year-old brain hadn't been expecting that. "Why does she hate him?"

"I don't know, but he said all girls are stupid." He looked away now. He looked uncomfortable.

"Do you think I'm stupid?"

"No," he said, looking at me again, and then down and

the ground before he said quietly, "But you didn't come with us yesterday."

"I didn't have a bike."

He nodded.

"Do you want to come over now? We can play in the fort. Sarah and Tilly aren't around." I smiled at him. Hoping to put this sorry affair to bed.

"No, Michael will call me a wimp if I play with girls." He turned away from the gate now, looking back at the ball he had left in the middle of the green lawn. "I'll see you." he said, without looking back at me.

IN OUR GARDEN, Emily and Christina were playing on scooters. "That's mine!" I said when I saw Christina.

"You weren't using it!" Christina exclaimed.

"Well, I am now!" I took it from her and started going up and down the garden.

"I'm going to tell Mum that you kissed John," Christina said angrily.

My stomach turned unpleasantly. I was terrified. I knew I would be in trouble. Mum had never really liked boys coming over to play. She was fine with Tilly and Sarah, but she didn't like the idea of John and Michael being over so often. I knew I was in trouble as I watched Christina run into the house.

"Do you think she really will?" I asked Emily.

"I don't know, but why don't you just lie about it and say you didn't." Emily suggested with a shrug of her shoulders.

Christina came running back outside as Emily was going up and down the garden on her scooter. I was standing where I had been when Christina left, awaiting my fate.

"Mum wants to talk to you." Christina grinned slyly at me, looking like the cat that got the cream. She knew I was in trouble. My stomach continued to churn. My mouth was dry and my palms were sweaty. I walked slowly up the concrete steps, my legs feeling like lead.

"Mum?" I called out, apprehensively from the door.

She was in the bath. I walked down the long corridor to the bathroom, not knowing what was going to come, but feeling sure that it was going to be bad. I shouldn't have kissed him. I knew that. It was stupid. I should have said no. I stood outside the brown door for a minute before pushing it open. Mum looked at me, half-submerged in the hot water.

"Is it true?" she said, looking at me. I couldn't read her tone but her face told me she was disappointed.

I felt the tears well in my eyes. They started to spill down my cheeks, hot with shame and guilt. "You're much too young to be doing that," she said. "You can't spend time with those boys again. I'll have to talk to your father about this, but until then, you're grounded."

I nodded, unable to speak for the shame and embarrassment I felt.

"Go to your room." Mum dismissed me without further discussion.

I left the bathroom and walked slowly down to the bedroom I shared with Christina and Emily. I sat on the side of the bed. I couldn't believe Christina had told her. I looked over to Christina's bed and wondered if I could do something to it to get back at her. 'I was so stupid for kissing him,' I thought, 'It was all Emily's fault! If she hadn't said anything it would never have happened.' I lay on the bed and forced myself to stop crying. It was all my own fault really. I shouldn't have said yes to being John's girlfriend. I should have refused to kiss him. I hated Christina for telling on me, but I shouldn't have done it. She was a telltale. I shouldn't have kissed him in the first place. I didn't deserve to be upset because it was all my own fault.

The next time I saw John, he was hiding, waiting for me to cycle down the lane behind his house, so he could squirt me with water from his pistol.

I never spoke to him again.

I feel Sick

I was sick. I knew I was sick before I even opened my eyes.

"Up you get!" Mum burst into the room and pulled back the curtains. The sunlight came pouring into the room.

"Ugh," Emily moaned from the bunk above me, "Go away."

"Are you not excited to get up? It's your Confirmation today!" Mum asked, standing by Christina's bed, "Jess, are you awake?"

"Yeah," I mumbled, rolling over, "I don't feel well."

"Oh, I'm sure you'll be fine. Get up and get some breakfast, you'll be alright." Mum left the room and I lay there feeling sick. My tummy hurt, and I could feel a burning sensation in my groin. Then suddenly I needed to pee. I jumped out of bed and ran down to the bathroom. I didn't need to go. That was weird. I came out of the bathroom and joined Christina in the kitchen for breakfast. There were bowls in the middle of the table with spoons and three boxes of cereal. I chose Cornflakes and poured them into my bowl.

"It's my Confirmation today!" Emily bounced into the

kitchen in her Pocahontas pyjamas and her long brown hair tangled from sleep.

"Hurry up and have your breakfast or there'll be no Confirmation," Dad was grumpy, as usual, "Have you had your cod liver oil?"

"Ugh! No!" Emily said dramatically, pushing him away on her way to the table.

"It's good for you." Dad grabbed the glass bottle from the cupboard and three big spoons. He came towards the table and Emily jumped up.

"I need water, I can't take that vile stuff on its own. It's disgusting!"

Dad turned to me. He poured the yellow oil onto the tablespoon and handed it to me. I scrunched up my face and put it in my mouth, swallowing the oily liquid quickly. "Ugh!" I said when it was over.

He then turned to Christina and the same thing happened. Finally, he turned to Emily. "Ugh!" she moaned as he poured her spoonful. She took it from him with her face scrunched in disgust and as soon as she swallowed, she gulped down her water. "That's so disgusting!" she declared to the room.

I still didn't feel well, but I forced myself to eat some breakfast. "Mum, I'm feeling really sick," I said when I was putting my bowl in the dishwasher.

Mum looked at me and put her hand on my forehead. "Well, you don't have a temperature. We have a few minutes before we really have to go, so why don't you go back to bed and see if you start to feel any better?" I nodded and went back to bed. I closed my eyes and let myself really feel sick. Breakfast had not helped. At all.

"What are you wearing?" Emily asked Christina loudly as they came back into our shared bedroom. I heard

Christina opening the wardrobe and taking out the clothes Mum had told her to wear. They proceeded to discuss the outfit Mum had chosen for Christina, and which shoes would go best with it, before they turned to what Emily was wearing. I heard the rustling of plastic bags and boxes as Emily's new outfit was taken out of its hiding place. Christina was appropriately awed by it, and I felt even more ill.

"What are you wearing, Jess?" Emily had obviously only now noticed that I was there.

"Why are you in bed?" Christina asked.

"I don't feel well," I replied, rolling over slowly.

"Are you coming to my Confirmation?" Emily was peering down at Jess now.

Rolling over had caused my head to start spinning so I waited until it stopped before I replied. "I don't know. I feel sick," I finally said.

GRANNY AND GRANDAD were meeting us at the church, but Aunt Jane came to the house before we left for church.

"Oh Emily, you look lovely!" Aunt Jane proclaimed. Emily had come into the sitting room and twirled around in her new red and black dress. She had black pumps and a black cardigan to go with it. She really did look lovely with her long hair tied back in a butterfly clip. I was sitting on the couch, still feeling ill, but dressed in my appointed outfit nonetheless.

"Are you okay, Jess?" Aunt Jane asked when she saw me.

"I feel sick," I said, feeling very sorry for myself.

"Oh no! That's such a pity," she looked at me with concern.

"She's coming to the mass, and we'll see how she feels afterwards," Emily told her.

Mum gave Aunt Jane a look and they both left the room. I put my head on the arm of the couch.

"You don't look good," Christina said.

"I don't feel well."

Aunt Jane drove Emily to the church, she was her godmother and always gave her special treatment because of it. She was also Emily's sponsor, so when we arrived at the church, they both disappeared to find the seat Emily had been assigned. Granny and Grandad pulled up in their car moments after us.

"You'll see her after the service. She wanted to make sure she was on time and found her seat," Mum explained to Granny when she asked where Emily was, "But you look lovely."

"Thank you, and Jess, that dress is very nice but are you okay?" Granny was looking at me now as I leaned against the car, breathing slowly.

I shook my head. "I'm not well. I feel really sick."

"We're going to see how she feels after the mass," Mum explained.

There were three schools being confirmed that day, that meant there would be sixty plus children and all of their relatives. The church and its grounds were teaming with people. We found an empty pew near the back of the church, and I sat between Granny and Christina. I thought the mass would never end, and I thought I might die in that pew with all of the people crowded around us and no fresh air. I just kept feeling more and more sick.

"May you go in peace," the priest finally said, after

what felt like days, and I stood up quickly, desperate to get outside into the fresh air.

"Are you okay?" Granny asked within an element of concern in her voice.

"I need to go outside," I replied, gripping onto the row of seats in front of us to keep from falling.

"We just have to wait until the children all go out first," Mum said, glancing over at me.

I thought I was going to cry. Or faint. I did neither though, I just sat down and tried to think of other things to take my mind off how ill I felt. Finally, after what felt like a lifetime, we were allowed to stand up and leave. Fresh air had never felt so good.

The teaming of people all around didn't cease. Everyone gathered outside the front of the church before making their way around to the hall at the back for refreshments. I held onto Mum's bag, so as not to lose her, and we let the people push past us. "It was such a lovely service, wasn't it?" One of the other mums was saying to Granny.

"Very nice. Is that the usual parish priest?" Granny asked.

"It is. Father John, a lovely man," the lady replied, "He gives such a nice service."

I was breathing really slowly now, to stop the nausea.

"Are you coming around to the hall?" the lady said to Granny.

"We'll be around in a few minutes," Granny smiled at her and waved her off as she started moving off towards the parish hall. We followed a minute later. The hall was full of children running around and parents standing in groups talking, drinking tea and eating biscuits. I took a cup of juice, hoping it would help me feel better. It did a bit so I risked a chocolate biscuit. We seemed to be onto a winner.

I wandered around the hall aimlessly, seeing if there was anyone I knew. I recognised Evelyn Murphy. Her sister, Michelle, was in Emily's class, and she was in mine, but we weren't really friends. I waved and smiled at her and she nodded in response.

Outside, there were more children, chasing each other on the grass or standing around their parents as the adults all talked together.

"That mass was soooo long!" Christina announced when she saw me.

"I thought it would never end." I said, taking another bite of biscuit.

"Do you feel better?" Christina seemed a little concerned at least. Nobody else had asked if I was any better.

"No," I replied, "Well, I feel better outside in the fresh air, and this is helping," I indicated to my drink. "But I still feel really sick."

"You look sick."

"That's lovely. Thank you," I replied sarcastically.

"Well, you do," Christina smiled back at me.

I don't know how long we stayed at the church but eventually it was decided that it was time to continue the Confirmation celebrations elsewhere. Granny, Grandad and Emily were going to drive with Aunt Jane to Killruddery House, and Mum, Dad, me and Christina would travel in the second car.

"I still feel really sick," I said when we were in the car. Mum and Dad shared a look. I could tell that they didn't know what to do with me. It would have been much easier if I wasn't complaining about not feeling well.

"Well, we can see how you feel when we get to Killruddery House," Mum finally said. I closed my eyes and leaned my head against the window. The cool glass felt good against my hot skin. When the car stopped, and I opened my eyes, I didn't feel any better.

Jane, Granny, Grandad and Emily were already there when we arrived in the carpark. We walked up to the house and found out that the next tour started in an hour so we had time to walk around the gardens. They were beautiful and expansive but I was feeling awful. I trailed along behind everyone else, I just wanted the day to be over. Maybe I would have found the tour interesting if I hadn't felt so bad, and if we hadn't had to stand the whole time. There were signs all around the house, and on the furniture, telling visitors not to sit on anything. I contemplated sitting on the floor at one point but a stern look from Granny told me it was a bad idea.

When the tour finished, we headed back outside. "That was really interesting," Emily said, "I can't believe it's so big!"

"Mum, I'm still feeling really sick," I said as we walked back towards the cars.

"Okay, well we'll see what we're going to do now and then we can make a plan." I trailed along behind everyone, just wanting to sit down. Grandad sat on a bench in the carpark as we discussed what was going to happen next. I've never felt such joy at seeing a bench before.

"I want to go to Marcello's," Emily said, referring to the only restaurant we ever went to when we ate out. I loved it there and sitting down for a few hours felt like it would be much easier than the house and garden tour had been.

"But Jess is sick," Mum said.

"I can call my brother and see if she can stay with his wife," Dad said, referring to his brother, Paul, who was Emily's godfather. He had been working all day so he couldn't come to the Confirmation mass. His wife Amy was quiet and always seemed reserved the few times I had met her. I never really got the impression that she liked us, and I had never spent any time alone with her.

"Is Paul coming to Marcello's?" Aunt Jane asked.

"Yes, but I don't know if Amy is going to, so maybe Jess can stay with her." Dad was looking for Uncle Paul's number in his phone now.

It was confirmed that Amy was not coming to Marcello's, so I could stay with her. Dad drove everyone to the restaurant before he took me to Uncle Paul's house to stay with Amy. "You're not feeling well, are you not?" Amy said to me as Dad and I went into the hallway.

I shook my head. The hallway was dark and narrow but it was warm. There was a light coming from the sitting room.

"Paul is already on the way to meet you," Amy said to Dad. She was a head smaller than Dad and was very thin with short blonde hair.

Dad left and I looked awkwardly at Amy. I felt bad that she had to stay here with me when she probably would have rather gone out to dinner.

"Do you want to lie on the couch?" she asked.

I nodded and followed her into the sitting room. She handed me a blanket as I sat down. It was blue with white stripes and it was soft. I slipped my shoes off and lay back on the couch. My head resting on a cushion.

"Do you want me to put the TV on?" she asked when I was settled.

I shook my head.

"She's asleep." I felt myself come to. I didn't know where I was, my surroundings felt confusing and new. The heavy blanket that covered me was stifling. I opened my eyes and remembered, it was Emily's Confirmation and I was in Paul and Amy's house.

"Did you sleep?" Dad was now talking to me.

"Yeah," I said sitting up.

"We should get out of your hair," Dad said to Amy and I stood up. Suddenly I felt uncomfortable. Something felt weird.

"Well, look after yourself," Amy said to me, "And I hope you feel better."

I had wet myself. I could feel my dress sticking to my legs. My stomach dropped. Oh God. Dad would be really angry with me if he knew. I would be in trouble for ruining the sofa. I couldn't say anything. I smiled at Amy and left. I sat in silence in the car, hoping that Dad didn't smell anything. I would be in trouble for not saying anything sooner. I would be in trouble for ruining the sofa and for ruining the car seats. I should have sat on a plastic bag to protect the seats. I should have used the bathroom. Tears started to well up in my eyes as the shame ate away at me. When Dad pulled into the drive I jumped out and ran into the house. I went to my room and quickly changed out of my wet, dirty clothes and went straight to bed.

I was taken to the doctor the next day. I had a kidney infection and put on antibiotics. I was off school for a week.

"WE GOT THE PHOTOS BACK!" Emily came running into the sitting room. "We got lots of photos but we got my Confirmation ones back!" Christina, Emily and I sat on the floor and Emily opened the first envelope. It wasn't what she was looking for so she moved onto the next one, until finally, she found her photos. "I look so nice!" she exclaimed, "That dress was really lovely!"

There were photos of her and Aunt Jane, her and Mum and Dad, her and Granny and Grandad, her and the priest and her teacher. There was one of all of us, but I was looking away and you couldn't really tell it was me in the photo. I found one of me, Grandad and Granny sitting on a bench in the carpark of Killruddery House, and I looked awful. My face was pale and I looked so ill.

I wondered if no one had known I was sick. Maybe I hadn't said it, or I hadn't said it enough, but when I saw that photo, I knew that I had said it enough and no one had listened to me.

My heart sank.

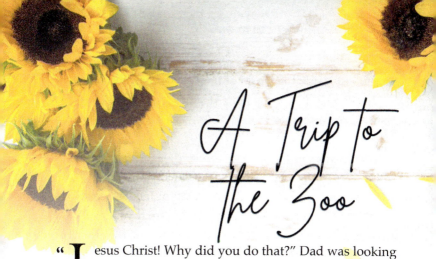

A Trip to the Zoo

"Jesus Christ! Why did you do that?" Dad was looking furious from his seat at the end of the table.

Jess jumped and ran to the sink to get the sponge. She was too small and she couldn't reach it. Grabbing a chair, she stood on it so she could get the sponge.

"Will you hurry up! The water is going everywhere!"

Sponge in hand, Jess ran back to the table and the mess she had created. She picked up the glass and started mopping up the water as it spread far and wide across the kitchen table.

"That was a fairly stupid thing to do, it's gotten everywhere!" her dad grumbled.

Jess ran from the table, back to the sink to squeeze out the excess water. Then she was back wiping up the last of the mess. The only things that were soaking wet were some placemats. Jess dried those off and put the sponge back in the sink.

"You won't do that again in a hurry!" Dad said, turning back to the newspaper he was reading.

I'm such an idiot, Jess thought, as she put the placemats back where they'd been. She looked over at her father, hoping he might notice that the table was now cleaner than it had been before but he was lost to her again; lost inside the world of politics and current affairs.

Back in her bedroom, her sister Emily was brushing her hair. "Are you ready to go? Mum said we're leaving in 5 minutes."

They were going to the zoo and Jess couldn't wait. They were going with Mum's friend Gillian and her three kids, David, Aiden and Annie. David and Aiden were eight and ten, and Annie was six, a year younger than Jess. Both Emily and Jess got on well with all of them. Today was going to be great!

"Right," Mum was standing by the front door, balancing the baby on one arm and the pram in the other arm. Emily picked up a bag from the floor that was filled with bread rolls, packets of ham and cheese, and fruit, and Jess picked up the other bag with drinks for the day.

"We'll see you later, Peter," Mum shouted to their father who was still in the kitchen. Dad didn't even realise that they were leaving.

Christina, at two years old, was still called the baby. She sat in a car seat beside the window, and Jess and Emily sat beside her. "Seatbelts on?" Mum asked from the front seat. The girls nodded and they set off.

At the zoo they parked and unloaded the car. All of the food went into the bottom of the buggy, while Christina climbed in. Mum gave a rucksack to each of the girls which had an extra jumper and water for each of them. "You need to hold onto the pram so you don't get lost," Mum instructed as they started walking towards the entrance of the zoo.

There were people milling around everywhere.

"There's Annie!" Jess shouted, pointing towards the other end of the car park, where she could see a small blonde girl with a red hat. She was wearing blue denim shorts and had a black t-shirt with a yellow star emblazoned on the front. Jess let go of the pram and started running towards her. Emily followed close behind. Annie's face lit up when she saw the girls. Gillian and the two boys were coming up close behind her, and they greeted Jess and Emily with hugs and smiles.

"I can't wait to see the alligators!" Aiden said, "I heard they're huge!"

"They don't have alligators," David replied, "They're crocodiles."

"I don't care what they're called, I just want to see their big teeth!" Aiden opened his own mouth wide to demonstrate.

The girls laughed as their mum came up with the buggy and the baby.

"Hi Julie," Gillian said, kissing Mum, "And you, little one!" She leaned over and looked into the pram. Christina was smiling away, looking around at everything around her, an old blanket clasped in her little hands.

"Are we ready to go in?" Mum looked around at everyone. They nodded and made their way to the entrance. There was a queue, but it wasn't a long wait until they were inside.

"Can we see the elephants first?" Emily asked.

"No, I want to go to the crocodiles!" Aiden chimed in.

"We'll follow the path around," Gillian told them, "We'll start over this direction and I think it should be a circle around." They started walking, looking at all of the different animals in their different habitats.

"I'm hungry," Annie announced suddenly.

"We have biscuits," Mum told her. She looked at Gillian, who nodded. They moved out of the flow of people and the pram was emptied out as the biscuits were searched for. Finally, they were found.

"Chocolate digestives! My favourite!" Aiden said.

Everyone got two biscuits each.

"Look at the lion over there," David exclaimed suddenly, "She's standing up!"

The four children stood and watched the lioness slowly get to her feet and start to walk around the outskirts of her enclosure. Christina sat in the pram sucking on the biscuit she had been given.

"She's moving so slowly," Aiden said, "I wonder if she's old."

"Or tired," Jess chimed in, "she was probably sleeping."

"What do the lions eat?" Annie asked.

"Monkeys," David replied, winking at his brother who was beside him.

"What?" Annie's little face looked distraught.

"The zookeepers take the monkeys from the enclosure and put them in with the lions so they can catch them and eat them," David continued.

"Don't be mean, David," his mother said in a warning voice, noting Annie's distraught face. "That's not true Annie, love. They feed them meat that's already dead." She shot a warning look at her oldest son who smirked.

"Are the monkeys nearby?" Annie asked.

"I'm not sure. Why don't we keep moving and see if we can find them." Everything was packed back into bags and the buggy and they kept walking.

"There they are!" Annie shouted excitedly.

The enclosure was a large caged area with plenty of space for the monkeys to climb and jump. All the children ran over to the enclosure and stood watching the little animals jump and swing, flying all over the cage. There was a big tree in the middle of the enclosure they were climbing up and down, and they had a separate wooden climbing frame they were using as well. Jess was looking at them in awe. They were so agile and looked to be having so much fun. One of the little ones was pulling at the tail of another monkey, and when he turned around, the trickster was hiding behind a bigger monkey, letting the bigger one take the blame.

"Look at that one stealing food from the hand of the other one," Jess giggled, nudging David beside her, but when she turned, she saw it wasn't David. It was another boy she didn't know, "Oh, I'm sorry!" She turned to her other side but Annie wasn't there either. Turning away from the enclosure, she looked around but she couldn't see anyone she knew. She couldn't see Mum, Emily or Christina, or Gillian. She felt herself start to panic. Where was everyone? She walked slowly away from the monkey enclosure, back onto the path they had been on.

Maybe she could find them if she just followed the path, but she soon realised that there were now two potential paths they could have taken. One path took them towards the elephant enclosure, the other went into the reptile house.

Standing in the middle of the path, Jess scoured the crowd, desperately looking for someone she recognised. There was no one. She could feel the panic moving up from her stomach and into her chest. The tears were starting to come. What was she going to do? But there was no point in crying, what were tears going to do? So, she walked back to the monkeys and stood against the fence watching them.

They would notice she was missing soon. They would

come back to look for her and find her if she stayed in the same spot. She clung onto the railing that ran around the monkey enclosure and willed herself not to cry.

"Mum, where's Jess?" Emily asked a few hours later.

"What?"

"Where's Jess?" Emily repeated, looking around and then back to her mother.

Julie looked around in a panic. "Where is Jess?"

Gillian looked at her friend. "When did you last see her?"

"Hang on a second," Julie replied. She looked around at all of the children, "One, two, three are yours and one and the baby...oh God! Jess?" Julie looked around her in a desperate panic now.

"She was beside me," David started to say and then he thought for a minute, "She was beside me at the monkeys," he finally finished, "She was definitely with us at the monkeys."

"That was ages ago!" Gillian said.

"That was before lunch," Julie replied, "Has she not been with us all this time?"

Jess was holding onto the railing so hard her hands were starting to hurt. Her feet already hurt and her stomach was grumbling but she wasn't going to move. They would come back for her; they would find her if she stayed in the same place. She knew they would. They would notice she was gone and they would come back for her. They had to.

The worst thing that could happen is that they won't notice until they're back in the car, she thought to herself, but in the car, it'll be really obvious that I'm not there.

"Jess!"

She turned around and let out a huge sigh of relief. It was Mum. She had come back. She had found her. "What are you doing?" Mum scolded her, "You were supposed to be holding onto the pram so you wouldn't get lost."

Jess wanted to cry with relief but she stopped herself.

"It was Emily who noticed you were missing. There are so many of you children that I had to count to see that we were missing anyone," Mum said, taking Jess's hand, "You should have been paying more attention." Jess followed after her mother, her body flooded with relief and firmly holding onto her hand, for fear she'd lose sight of her again.

"There you are!" Gillian exclaims when she sees Jess and Julie returning. All four children run up to meet them.

"Where were you?" Michael asked, "We were looking everywhere for you!"

"She stayed behind at the monkeys," Mum replied, rolling her eyes at her friend, "I told them to hold onto the pram so they didn't get lost."

"But at least we found you again," Julie said, smiling down at Jess, "Are you hungry? You must be starving! You missed lunch."

"I don't know if there's anything left," Emily said, looking into the pram.

Two biscuits and an apple were found. Jess was starving but just felt so relieved to be back that she hardly noticed.

Emily talked the whole way home about all of the

animals she had seen. A lot of them Jess had missed so she sat quietly, looking out the window.

"Jess got lost," Emily announced to their father when they got home.

Her dad looked at her questioningly. "Why did you do that?"

Jess shrugged, "I looked around and everyone was gone. I didn't know where they'd gone."

"She should have been paying more attention," Mum said.

Christmas and it's Devastations

"Oh my God Jess, do you remember that time you cried because your teacher was leaving? What a weirdo!"

It was Christmas Eve and we were on our annual visit to the Conlon's. We were all sitting around their kitchen table - all five of us, and seven out of ten of them. The little ones were already asleep. Emily was on the far side of the table from me. I had been talking to Caitríona about school when her jeering tone stopped me in my tracks. I knew this question well. I had heard it often, in mostly similar settings, and I knew the answer well. The answer was no. No, I don't remember this incident, but I do remember all of the times that Emily laughed at me about it. I remember everyone around us laughing at me, too. I remember her jeering and mocking me, and everyone looking and laughing.

The incident took place when I was eight years old. I was just finishing first class and our teacher, who I remember had thick blonde hair and was so kind to me, was leaving the school. I was devastated. This was the teacher that had allowed me to come into her classroom mid-year, despite the fact that there were already thirty-one children in her class. I remember standing in the corridor where we were picked up, and I remember Emily telling me I cried but I don't remember the incident myself.

I remember being laughed at for it, and everyone joining in, and no one stopping it. I remember Mum and Dad being there every time she did it and them allowing it to happen. I remember having no one to stop it or protect me so I remember laughing along, too.

Every time Emily brought it up again, every time I was laughed at for crying, I had the same thoughts 'What an idiot I was. A stupid weirdo crying over a teacher that didn't know me, a teacher that made me feel safe and wanted. How could I have been so stupid because if she had really known me, she wouldn't have wanted me. How could she, no one was interested in me so why would this teacher be?'

But maybe Santa would. This big fat man they all talked about. He wore red and lived far away, but he knew what we were doing all the time, maybe he would care. He had to care, why would he bring me presents every year if he didn't?

Maybe Santa could protect me. I needed him to. I needed to feel loved and wanted by someone. I was ten years old and I needed Santa to be real. I could tell him things and he wouldn't laugh at me. He wouldn't make fun of me and he would listen to me. I wrote letters to him as if he was real, but there was something niggling in the back of my head and in the school playground, telling me that he wasn't real. I needed him to be. But as Sarah McGrath said, a man flying around the world in one night did sound fanciful, but it also sounded incredible. It would mean that magic was real and that sounded cool, too. Someone that cared about me and would listen to me and magic all true if Santa was real.

But Sarah and the doubt were really doing a number on me. And with the doubt came the devastation. What did I have left if it wasn't true? Who did I have in my corner if there was no Santa?

I needed to find out. Not knowing was killing me.

It was November. I wrote my letter to Santa as usual. I told him things I couldn't tell my parents, and I thanked him for listening. I wrote out my list, sealed the envelope and dropped it into the letterbox on the way to school.

My plan was in action.

"What did you ask Santa for?" Mum was asking us all at dinner.

"A Chuckie doll," I said.

"Is that it?" She looked surprised. Our lists were usually extensive.

"I asked for other things too, but I've told Santa."

"And you're not going to tell anyone else?" Mum had put down her fork and was looking at me now.

"No." I replied and continued to eat my lasagna.

I waited with bated breath for Christmas morning. I was terrified to know the truth, but I needed to know. What would I get? Would he get me the Polly Pocket I had asked for as well?

"Wake up! It's Christmas! Santa's been!" It was 4am and Emily was already awake, and going through her pile.

I looked at mine and saw Chuckie sitting on top. He was so cool. My absolute favourite Rugrat because he was so openly a scaredy cat, but he always went along with Tommy's adventures anyway. So maybe that meant he wasn't really a scaredy cat but they just told us that he was, and so we believed it.

Underneath Chuckie was a Pocahontas jigsaw and a colouring book with gel pens and colouring pencils. My red stocking was stuffed with crisps and sweets and some stickers for my school books and a bouncing ball. There was no Polly Pocket. There was nothing else from my list besides Chuckie.

My stomach dropped. It was an unpleasant feeling that I knew well, and I hated it. This time, it represented the devastation, despair, and the disappointment I was feeling at finding out that Santa Clause was, in fact, not real. It had been my parents all along. I had never really had anyone I could talk to, or anyone I could write to, who would listen. It had all been a lie and the rising feeling of sadness was almost unbearable to hold.

"Let's go and wake up Christina, and see what she got!"

Emily was already finished with her pile and needed to go through someone else's things.

I stuffed my rising emotions down and followed her out of the room. There was no time to be sad or disappointed. It was Christmas and no one wanted to see my sadness or disappointment. I put on a smile to tell Mum about all of the things I had received. I smiled when Aunt Jane brought Granny over and Seán gave us the obligatory book we got every year. All of my negative emotions were squashed down because it was Christmas, and I had presents. I should be happy, shouldn't I? Just because the magical man wasn't real, who cares? Everyone knew he wasn't real anyway; didn't Sarah McGrath say that?

Later that day, the fire was lit, Harry Potter was playing on the TV and Christina walked in from the playroom.

"Is Santa real?" she asked me.

"No," I said.

I stood up and I left the room.

"AND YOU TOLD me he wasn't real on Christmas Day! I can't believe you told me on Christmas Day. I was devastated." The only thing that was ever mentioned about that Christmas was Christina's disappointment. Christina's devastation about finding out about Santa and she said it was made all the worse because I told her on Christmas Day. Why couldn't I have lied to her? Why did I tell her?

"That wasn't very nice of you," Mum said, "Why couldn't you have pretended?"

I never told anyone about my own devastation. I had learnt a long time ago that no one listened to me, no one wanted to know how I was, and if I told them they said to stop being so silly. I knew my devastation would fall on deaf ears, so I never told anyone. Instead, I listened to how I had ruined Christmas for Christina on that Christmas Day because I had answered her question honestly, amidst my own heartbreak and sadness.

I never told anyone that I had lost the only support and person who had cared for me on that day too.

I Led Him On

> Michael: Are you at home?

> Jess: No. I'm away for the weekend.

> Michael: Oh, very good. Where are you?

> Jess: In Galway. Staying with my friend. I came down for the Arts Festival

> Michael: That's nice. So ye're going out tonight?

> Jess: Yes. There's a show in the Black Box and we're leaving soon.

> Michael: Oh, very nice. What are you wearing? ;)

I sat up suddenly. I looked at the message again. Was it real? Oh God. Michael was the handyman that Dad used around the house. I had known him for years but he was in his forties and married, so far as I knew anyway.

"Jess! Are you ready?" I jumped off the bed and ran downstairs. Louise was standing by the door in shiny purple leggings and an orange blouse. She was putting on her black fur coat and her bleached blond hair was high on her head in a bun. "You look lovely," she smiled at me, "I love the dress." My little black dress paled in comparison to her bright, vibrant outfit but I smiled.

Louise's husband Dave came out to the hall. "We all ready, then?"

I nodded, following them both out of the house and into the car. I didn't say much as we drove through Galway to the Black Box Theatre. I couldn't get Michael's message out of my head. It made me feel so uncomfortable, but I didn't know if I should. Maybe it wasn't meant the way I was taking it.

As soon as we were out of the car and it was just Louise and I, I showed her the message. "Who is this guy?" she asked, looking at my phone.

"My dad's friend. Well, he does work around the house."

"That's disgusting!" Louise was clearly appalled, and I felt validated. "How old is he?"

I shrugged, "In his forties, maybe."

"No, absolutely not," Louise said, handing me back my phone. "That is not okay. You should tell your dad. What does he think he's doing with messages like that to a twenty-year-old? And his friend's daughter. Absolutely not!"

I sighed with relief. I wasn't overreacting.

> Michael: How was the show last night?

I WAS ON THE BUS, on the way back to Dublin, the next day. I hadn't replied to Michael's message from the day before.

I had managed to put it out of my mind and had a blast at the gig with Louise and afterwards, we went dancing. I was exhausted and didn't want to read any more weird messages from him.

But if I was honest, I liked the attention he was giving me. I liked texting him, but I also knew he was being really inappropriate. I had been relieved when Louise told me that what he had said wasn't okay. I wasn't overreacting. But now here he was again and I didn't know what to do.

> Jess: It was good. A really fun night

> Michael: Are you staying in Galway for a while?

> Jess: No just the weekend. I'm on the way home now.

> Michael: Great. I might be over to the house tomorrow. Not sure of the time. I'll let you know and see if you're there to let me in.

> Jess: That's grand. Just let me know.

> Michael: Are you out tonight?

> Jess: No. I was out last night. I'm wrecked!

> Michael: Was it a good one then?

> Jess: Really good. We went to a club in town.

> Michael: Very nice! Did you kiss any boys? ;)

Jess: I might have.

> Michael: You don't want to tell me?

Jess: It's none of your business ;)

> Michael: No, I suppose it isn't. But I would like it if it was

I THREW the phone down and looked at it. Oh God! I was definitely leading him on. What was I doing? What should I do now? I could feel the guilt start to seep in. He may have been inappropriate before, but now it was my fault for leading him on. I could feel the shame start to rise and mix with the guilt.

The next morning, I decided I wouldn't reply to any more of his messages. If I ignored him, he would have to go away, wouldn't he?

"Ann, are you free to get Korean food tonight?" I was in the college canteen and I suddenly really wanted Korean food. My friend, Ann, was half way through her cheese and chicken toastie beside me.

"I have a lecture until six tonight, but I can go afterwards. Are you thinking of the place in Parnell Square?"

"Yeah, that's always really good. I'll text around and see if anyone else is free."

In the computer room, I logged onto my account and went into my free online text messages.

Jess: Going for Korean food at 6.30 tonight if you want to come. Meet at the Spire.

And I hit send.

> Michael: I'm afraid I'm not free.

My stomach lurched. Oh God. I had sent it to Michael Jameson instead of my friend Micheál Deery.

> Jess: Whoops. That wasn't meant for you!

> Michael: You didn't want to invite me?

> Jess: I don't think it's really your scene.

> Michael: I suppose not. I don't really like hot food.

> Jess: It's very hot, probably best for you to steer clear.

> Michael: Well, I hope you don't burn your tongue!

> Jess: I'll do my best.

Bullet dodged, I thought. Ugh! What was I doing? I couldn't delete his number because Mum and Dad would think that was weird. The only reason he had my number in the first place was so I could let him into the house when he was coming over to fix things. I remembered what Louise had said about telling Dad. I had immediately dismissed the idea when she said it. Dad wouldn't listen. And I didn't want to cause a fuss. He was working for Dad and I didn't want to make it awkward for him. I didn't know how it would be fixed and it would be so weird. And sure, I was leading him on anyway.

I MET ANN, Cian and Carla at the Spire that evening and we walked up to Kimchi Hophouse on Parnell Street. The restaurant was busy, as usual, but we got a table and we ordered food. It was a really fun night and a great way to catch up with people. Afterwards Ann and I walked towards home together.

My phone pinged.

Michael: *How is your tongue?*

I stopped walking and stared at it.

"What?" Ann looked back at me, "What is it?"

I showed her the message. She looked confused.

"Who's Michael?"

"My dad's friend."

Her eyes widened with surprise. "Your dad's friend is asking you about your tongue?"

I nodded. "I accidentally sent him a message inviting him tonight," I looked at the ground ashamed. "He's been sending me really weird messages."

"How weird?" Ann looked at me with curiosity and apprehension.

"He asked me what I was wearing when I was at Louise's," I replied.

Ann's face told me that she thought the same as Louise.

"I don't know what to do," I said with desperation.

"Have you told your dad?"

"No, I haven't told anyone."

Ann looked at my phone again. "Maybe you could just tell him to stop?"

"You think that'll work? I don't want it to be weird because of the work he does with Mum and Dad."

"But he shouldn't be sending you messages like that.

That's really inappropriate." Ann was looking down at my phone again.

"So, what do I do?"

"Do you think your dad would get him to stop?"

"I don't want to tell him. It'll make everything weird because he's working for dad. I just want him to leave me alone," I said miserably.

"Why don't we send him something and just see if we can get him to leave you alone," she suggested.

"Sure," I said, hesitantly but willing to try anything at this point.

She looked down at my phone for a minute. Then she started typing before handing the phone back to me.

I don't think my dad would think these kinds of messages to his daughter are very appropriate.

"What do you think?" she asked looking at me, "Does it sound OK?"

"Yeah, it does." I looked at Ann, took a deep breath and pressed send.

"Okay. That's it. It's done. Ugh! Why does this happen? Why can't he just not be a creep and leave me alone?"

Ann linked her arm with mine, "I know! It's so weird."

We hadn't moved five steps before my phone pinged again.

"Oh God."

I handed Ann the phone. She read the message and scoffed.

Michael: *You didn't seem worried about that before but you're probably right.*

"What a load of shit!" she said, "Trying to blame you but at least it's over now."

I nodded, but of course I couldn't agree with her. I had

led him on but I wasn't going to tell her that. I was too ashamed to tell her.

THE NEXT DAY, I went into the kitchen where Mum was making a cup of tea. "Can I tell you something?" I asked awkwardly.

She looked surprised, "This sounds serious."

I looked at my feet, afraid to say anything, but Louise was right, I should tell one of them, and now that I'd dealt with it maybe things wouldn't be weird, "Michael Jameson has been sending me weird messages," I finally mumbled.

"What kind of weird messages?" I couldn't tell how she felt. Her face was completely blank.

"He asked me what I was wearing."

Mum didn't move. She stared at me for a minute.

"Right," she finally said, "Erm." she looked away, "When did this happen?"

"When I was at Louise's in Galway. He was texting asking if I was at the house, and when I said I was away he asked where, and then he asked what I was wearing."

Mum looked really uncomfortable.

"I don't know really," she said, "I don't know what to say."

I didn't respond. I didn't know what to say either.

"I don't know what to do," she picked up her cup now, "He's so good at his job. It's so hard to find a handyman that actually shows up when he says he will."

I stood where I was, still not knowing what to say. This was messing everything up. It was going to be weird now.

Michael was needed around the house to fix things and because they now knew I was uncomfortable it was going to make everything awkward. I shouldn't have said anything.

"Have you told your dad?" Mum asked and I shook my head.

"Maybe you should tell him."

I followed her up to the office, where Dad was standing by the window reading a document.

"Dad?"

He looked up when I came in. "Are you going to take a look at those policies I left out?" he asked gruffly.

"No, I'm not working today," I replied. I was already nervous but now I felt worse.

"Why not?" he looked at me in surprise.

"Because I'm not. Michael Jameson's been sending me weird messages," I blurted out in a rush.

"What weird messages?" Dad was looking at me now.

"He asked what I was wearing." I was looking at the floor now. Wishing I hadn't said anything.

Dad paused for a moment. "What's wrong with that?" he finally said.

"It made me feel really uncomfortable," I said, feeling that same discomfort again.

"But there's nothing wrong with asking what you're wearing."

Mum was now sitting at her desk working, as if we weren't even there. I looked at her for support. She didn't look up. "Okay," I finally said.

Later that day, Mum came into the kitchen where I was reading. "How are you feeling?" she asked.

I looked up, surprised. "I'm fine."

"That's good," she said brightly. After a few minutes she spoke again. "Maybe when Michael comes over again, you could make sure you're in your room. I'll text you if I know he's coming, but if we don't know and you see him you could just go into your room."

Talk To Your Cousins

"We're stopping here." Dad turned the car into the driveway facing out onto Clew Bay. The driveway is at an awkward angle so even before the words are said everyone knows where they are going.

"But I don't want to."

"It's boring."

"They don't talk to us." The words came as a chorus from the back seat.

"It's my brother," Dad says, "I want to see my brother."

He parks the car at the bottom of a sharp incline and turns off the engine.

"Can you not at least drive up?" Christina asked.

"We need to save petrol."

THE WORDS ARE SAID with an air of mischievousness but everyone knows that he isn't joking. 'Many a true word is said in gest' as he himself always says. Anything he can do to save money will be done, no matter how much anyone protests.

The three girls; Christina, Jess and Emily get out of the

car reluctantly and walk up the steep incline to the big black iron gates. "Did you press the bell?" Mum asks as she brings up the rear.

Jess nods. She doesn't want to climb over the wall but even before she pressed the bell, she knew it was in vain.

Jess, Christina and Emily played rock, paper, scissors to see who would have to climb over the wall this time. Dad beats them to it. He climbed over and disappeared around the corner, up to the house to let them know they have arrived so someone can open the gate.

"Why do we always have to stop here?" Emily complains.

"Your dad wants to see his brother," Mum responds.

"But why do we all have to suffer just because of what he wants?" Christina said, "He doesn't even stay. He leaves us here with no one to talk to because they don't want to see us," she gestures towards the house.

"That's not true," Mum says defensively.

Her daughters give her withering looks. They are all remembering their last visit when their aunt made them tea and then went into town to meet her sister, leaving them alone in the house. They found out later that two of their cousins had been upstairs the whole time but didn't bother coming down to say hello.

"It's so cold!" Emily said suddenly, stamping her feet to keep warm.

"Is it starting to rain?" Christina held her hand out and felt the large raindrops landing on it. The three girls and their mother moved closer to the trees that lined the driveway, hoping to shelter from the rain when the gate suddenly clanged.

"Oh, thank God!"

. . .

They waited for the gate to open wide enough and the three girls ran towards the house, leaving their mother to walk up behind them. Emily and Christina ran towards the back door and Jess ran towards the front. No one tried the conservatory, even though it was usually unlocked. The dog was in the conservatory and it wasn't a nice dog. Jess rang the doorbell and leaned against the wall panting. The rain was coming down harder now. They were lucky the gate had been opened when it had. She stood looking at the big raindrops falling and wondered how long it would take someone to open the front door. The back door would have been a better idea. Five minutes later Jess pressed the doorbell again, and Christina opened it. The two girls rolled their eyes at each other and Jess followed her sister into the kitchen.

"There you are!" Dad said. He was sitting on a chair at the kitchen table. Aunt Máire was at the sink filling the kettle.

"Hello!" she said brightly, turning to the girls as they came in, "How are things?"

"Good," Emily replied just as brightly, "Are you here on your own?"

"No, no. Aoife is upstairs and I think Darragh is in the front room."

No one was surprised that neither of their cousins came out to say hello.

"Well, ye've arrived!" Uncle Brendan came into the room. He went over to his brother and shook his hand. "Did you not bring the Missus?" he asked, looking around surprised.

"Mum's coming now," Jess said.

"Are ye in the area for a few days?" Brendan asked, sitting beside his brother at the table.

"Oh, you know yourself, we're down to see the mother and the girls wanted to see their cousins," Dad replied.

"You should go into the front room. I'm sure Darragh would love to see you," Aunt Máire said.

Jess opened her mouth to protest but she couldn't think of anything to say so she looked at her sisters. Christina shrugged and stood up. Emily didn't move. Jess followed Christina out to the hall. "Should we just stand here for a while?" Jess asked.

"I have a better idea." Christina opened the door to the front room and stuck her head in. "Hi Darragh, your mum told us to tell you we're here and she's making tea if you'd like some."

Her cousin looked up from the TV he had been staring at in surprise. "Eh, okay," he finally said. Christina waited for him to say something else, and when he didn't, she backed out of the room and closed the door.

"Darragh said he'd be in in a minute," Jess told her aunt back in the kitchen.

She sat beside Mum who had just arrived in from the rain and Jess sat down across from her.

"Nice one," she whispered.

"Oh Aoife, look who's arrived," Aunt Máire exclaims. A sullen looking fifteen-year-old had just come into the kitchen.

"Oh right," she said looking around at the visitors, "Mam, can I get a lift into town?"

"Now?" Máire looked surprised.

"You said you would. Siobhán and Paula are already in there,"

"Maybe later,"

"But Mam!" Aoife is not impressed and Christina, Jess and Emily wondered if they were going to witness the full-on tantrum that had been a regular feature in Aoife's younger days.

"I can bring you in," Uncle Brendan suddenly said, "I'll only be gone a minute."

"So, how's school?" Aunt Máire asked after her husband and daughter left.

"Good. I got a part in the musical," Emily said.

"Very good. Which musical are you doing?"

"My Fair Lady. I'm Mrs Higgins, the main character's mother."

"That's great. You'll have to tell us when it's on. And are there any boyfriends?"

"Are your neighbours selling the house?" Dad wasn't interested in school talk and he definitely didn't want to hear about boyfriends.

"They are. They put it up two weeks ago. I don't know how much interest they've had so far." The talk turned to who was living where and what was happening locally. The girls sat quietly drinking their tea and looking aimlessly around the room.

"Why don't you three join Darragh in the front room," Mum suddenly said to them. Darragh, unsurprisingly, hadn't appeared in the kitchen.

"Because we don't want to," Christina said.

"Will you go in and say hello to your cousin!" Dad was getting cross.

"We did say hello to him. He said he'd be out in a minute," Christina replied, matching her father's anger.

"Where are the rest of them?" Dad now turned to Aunt Máire who was watching the spectacle play out.

"Caoimhín had a match and should be back soon, and Deirbhle is out with a friend."

"Traffic in town is really bad. There is a big crowd at

the O'Malley funeral. They're burying him tomorrow but the place looked packed for the wake." Uncle Brendan was back from dropping Aoife to her friends.

"Which O'Malley is that?" Dad loved hearing about the local news and he wouldn't miss a funeral. It was a great way to find out what had happened locally and he would meet people he hadn't seen in years. Everyone now knew what they would be spending the following morning doing.

Jess rested her head on her folded arms on the table. "Will you go in to Darragh," Mum hissed at her.

Deciding there was no use in arguing, she stood up. At least in the front room she would be able to sit quietly, because Darragh wasn't going to bother her, she thought. Christina followed her sister out, not wanting to be left discussing the latest of the O'Malley brothers that had died. Emily didn't move.

THE TWO GIRLS opened the door to the front room to find it empty. The TV screen was a frozen image of a football game. Darragh had obviously been playing with the PlayStation but he was now nowhere to be seen. Christina flopped down onto the sofa and Jess went over to the controller on the couch and picked it up.

"I wonder how you - oh! There you go." The screen came alive again and Jess pressed the different buttons to see what would happen. She eventually got control of the little men on the screen and ran up and down the pitch, trying to see where the ball was.

"It's down there, on the left," Christina said, joining in now, "It's got the little yellow arrows around it. Not over that side!"

"What are you doing?" Darragh was back and he was pissed. Jess looked at him just as the other team scored a goal on the screen. "You're ruining it!" He ran over to her and took the controller out of her hand, "My team are going to lose! What have you done?!" He was really angry now. He pushed Jess out of the way and sat down, pressing buttons on the controller furiously.

"I'm sorry. I was just messing around," Jess said stepping away from him, "Your mum told us to come in and talk to you, but you-"

"If I wanted to talk to you, I would have come out, wouldn't I? Jesus! You've ruined my streak!"

Jess looked at Christina, who shrugged and was thinking that the conversation about the dead O'Malley might have been a better option.

Jess stood awkwardly where she was and looked at her sister, "Do we go back out to the kitchen?"

Christina shrugged just as Darragh's older brother, Caoimhín, came into the room. "Oh!" Caoimhín looked surprised to see the two girls.

"Hi," he said and then turned to his brother, "It's my turn now."

"No, it's not, I'm not finished. Jess ruined my game so I get more time."

"No, you don't, it's my turn!"

"I have to finish this one because if I don't, I'll have lost my streak. It's Jess's fault, you can blame her," Darragh didn't take his eyes from the screen. His hands were furiously pressing buttons and he was glaring at the screen.

"For God's sake!" Caoimhín was now angry. He glared at Jess, "Why did you do that?"

"I didn't do anything! No one was playing when I came in. All I did was turn it on," Jess said defensively.

Caoimhín sat on the other end of the couch grumpily.

Jess was still standing. "I'm going to ask Mum if we can leave," she said to her sister.

Christina looked around to see if there was a book she could read, a magazine, an anything to pass the time.

"Dad's gone!" Jess was at the door, "And he's taken the car."

Family Obligations

"Are we nearly there?" Christina called from the back seat.

"Nearly," Mum replied dryly.

Jess knew her mother didn't even believe it herself. They were on the way to their cousin's First Holy Communion. It started at eleven and was a three hour drive to get there. Dad didn't want to spend extra money on accommodation so they had had to leave before 7am and everyone was feeling tired. Jess wasn't looking forward to the Communion. It was the third First Holy Communion in this same family of cousins and if the others had been anything to go by, this wasn't an event to be excited about. She looked down at *Mariel of Redwall*, the book she had started just as they left Dublin and began reading.

"You're still reading those books?" Emily was leaning over to get a look at the book title. Jess didn't reply. "You do know they're for kids, right? They're about mice and rabbits."

"They're hares," Jess said, "And they're really cool. They go on adventures and protect Redwall Abbey."

"They're for children, and you should really choose books that are for your own age."

Jess put the book up to her face, to hide her sister's

smug smile and tried to read. She had loved the *Redwall* books since she had first found them in the local library when she was in primary school. She loved the adventures the animals went on and that they always protected each other. She loved the descriptive feasts and landscapes and she loved the different ways each animal had of speaking. *Redwall* were some of her favourite books but her sister never let her enjoy them in peace, even when she was reading at night before bed. Emily insisted on mocking her, but Jess wouldn't give them up. She loved getting lost in the world of Mossflower Woods and even her sister's jeering tones wouldn't stop that.

An hour and a half later, Dad was pulling into a hotel car park. Everyone got out, took their pre-prepared bags of Communion clothes with them and went into the hotel bathrooms to change. Ten short minutes later and everyone looked more presentable and felt slightly more awake.

The Communion mass was long. Readings were read, thank yous were said, and everyone received the Body of Christ before the priest finally said, 'go in peace', which was the sign that everyone could leave. Outside the church, Jess, Christina and Emily stuck to each other. Everyone around them seemed to know everyone else.

"Oh hi," said Aoife, the sister of the Communion maker when she saw them, "Did you just get here?"

"Yes," Emily replied, "Just before the mass started. We came down this morning."

Aoife nodded and smiled. "Oh! I have to go and talk to someone," she suddenly said, looking over their heads, "Are you coming back to the house?"

Emily nodded and Aoife was gone.

Finally, Dad had spoken to all of the people he wanted

to talk to and herded his children back to the car, so they could go out to the cousins' house to continue the celebrations. Jess wasn't looking forward to this part. If they thought that Aoife walking off on them had been bad, wait until everyone walked off on them.

"Oh my God, what's that on your face?" All of the cousins had been put into the sitting room. They were given food, and the TV was on and the door was closed. There were Jess and her sisters, the four cousins of the family that were hosting the Communion, including Aoife and eight other cousins from the other side of the family, who all lived locally. Aoife's younger sister, Deirbhle, was scrutinising Jess's face. Jess could feel her cheeks reddening.

"Is that a moustache?" Deirbhle continued, "Your upper lip is so hairy."

Jess' stomach sank. She looked down at her plate and took another bite to have something to do. A few of the cousins from the other side of the family were looking at her. She wished Deirbhle would shut up. Deirbhle was laughing now.

"You should really wax that," she said.

Today was worse than had been expected, and they had only arrived at the house half an hour ago. Jess thought back to when she had asked Dad if she had to go to the Communion.

"It's your cousin, of course you have to go," was the only thing that was said about it. There was no question, just a command.

This was why she hadn't wanted to come. The moustache comment was the most Deirbhle had said to her since they had arrived. In the bathroom later, Jess examined her upper lip. It was hairy. She had thought that herself a while ago but hadn't thought too much about it. Now it was obviously time to do something about it. She would have to ask Mum what to do. She knew that men shaved their faces so maybe she could look into that, or maybe that wasn't a thing women did. Mum would know.

After she came out of the bathroom, she was told that everyone was on the trampoline outside. Jess loved trampolines and rushed outside to join them. There were four children bouncing when she got there so she stood to the side and waited for her turn. The group that were already waiting were all talking when she got there, and when they saw her they stopped. Jess stood a way off from them and looked at her feet.

Christina came running out then. "Are you waiting?" she asked her sister when she saw her.

Jess nodded. The others looked at them and then went back to whispering together in a group. Christina looked at Jess and was clearly feeling as unwelcome as she was. Finally, the others finished on the trampoline and Jess ran over to it.

"It's not your turn!" one of the group that had been whispering told her. She stopped, one foot on the ladder and one on the ground.

"Jack was waiting before you. He'd just gone to get something to eat."

Jess looked at a boy who had just walked up. "But, I was here first," she tried to say but no one was listening. Christina looked at her and shrugged.

They waited for two more groups that had 'been there before them' before they got their own ten minutes on the trampoline. Christina was convinced that their ten minutes was shorter than everyone else's, but there was no way to prove it, and even if they had been able to, no one was listening to them anyway.

Finally, after what felt like days, Dad announced that they were leaving. Jess was the first out the door. She leaned against the car waiting for the rest of her family to join her, and thought about how glad she was that the whole sorry affair was over.

"We're going to visit Jim and Evelyn," Dad announced as he pulled out of the cousin's driveway.

"Aw no!" Emily said.

"But Jim always comes out with some homophobic comment!" Jess said.

"I don't want to," Christina added.

"He's your uncle," Dad said, "You have to go."

"He's your father's brother," Mum added.

"So long as you don't disappear with the car!" Emily said, "If you leave us there again, I'm never going back again!"

Forty minutes later, Dad pulled up in front of a white, one-story bungalow. Jim and Evelyn lived on the farm that Dad had grown up on. As Jim was the oldest boy in the family, he had inherited it. Dad loved coming back and looking round the farm, walking across the hills, finding out what Jim was up to while he left his children and wife to talk to Jim's wife, Evelyn. Evelyn was fine, but she was deadly boring. She could make a short story about going to the shops, a long, long story that no one ever thought would end.

"Welcome, welcome!" Evelyn said as they all entered the house, "Were you down for the Communion? We couldn't go, unfortunately. We have Kate here and we just couldn't leave her."

"How is she doing?" Dad asked after his mother.

"She's doing okay. She just has a cold at the minute and I didn't want to leave her in case she needed me."

Dad disappeared down the corridor to the room where his mother was. Everyone else went into the front kitchen and sat at the table that took up most of the room.

"I'll put on the kettle," Evelyn announced.

"Oh no, don't do that, we have eaten and drunk everything we could ever need!" Mum said, but Evelyn was gone into the back kitchen to make tea and see what other food she could offer her guests.

"How is school?" she asked the room when she returned.

"It's good," Emily said, "Our hockey team got into the semi-finals this year."

"Oh, that's very good!"

"The final is on Thursday and the whole school is coming out to watch it."

Evelyn made the tea and laid out the table with slices of homemade brown bread, cheese and tomatoes. Mum eyed everyone around the table, warning them to eat. Dad was nowhere to be seen.

"Has he gone off with the car?" Emily whispered furiously to Jess, who only shrugged.

"The car is still outside," Christina announced as she came in from the bathroom, "He's probably just gone up to the shed with Uncle Jim."

"I think they have," Evelyn joined in, coming in from the back kitchen with slices of cake. Jess looked pleadingly at her mother. Mum wasn't as insistent that they ate the cake. She was obviously feeling over full herself and needing to do what was right by her sister-in-law wasn't seeming as possible anymore.

"Were there many at the Communion?"

"All of Máire's sisters were there with their kids," Mum said, "And all of Jim's brothers came, but they didn't bring their children. They all seem to be doing exams or have important matches." Christina eyed Jess across the table and Jess shrugged. They were both remembering the blazing row between Christina and Dad, because Christina's best friend was playing in the quarter final, but Dad refused to let her go because of the Communion.

"You'll never guess who came to visit us last week!" Evelyn suddenly said, "I was down at the shops and I ran into Biddy from over the road, you remember her, don't you?" This was the beginning of a long story. Jess could feel it coming but was powerless to stop it. It was a story everyone had heard before. Evelyn was going to tell them about Imelda May and her visit to the area. She was going to talk about her wearing stiletto heels into a field.

"And her heels sank right into the mud!" she finally said, signalling the end of the never-ending story. "I bet she was mortified. I was mortified for her!" Everyone around the table had smiles plastered onto their faces.

"Do you have the car keys?" Emily asked her mother when Evelyn had disappeared into the back kitchen again. Mum shook her head and all three children groaned. Dad had gone off with the car key. This wasn't the first time, and they knew it wouldn't be the last. They were stuck here, in the middle of nowhere with an old woman who couldn't get out of bed and a boring woman who couldn't remember when she had told the same story three times, and they knew they wouldn't be leaving anytime soon.

What felt like hours and hours later, the back door opened and Uncle Jim came in. "Well," he said, as if he wasn't expecting his nieces to be there, "You're very welcome!" He went around the kitchen table shaking everyone's hands. He called Emily, Jess, and Jess, Emily. Christina was sitting in the chair at the head of the table but when Uncle Jim came in, she moved. No one but Uncle Jim could sit at the head of the table.

The Six One News had started on the TV in the corner. "Sssshhh!" Uncle Jim said from his prime seat. He gestured with his arm for the volume to be turned up. Evelyn scurried to get the remote and higher the sound. Dad found a seat beside the TV and everyone sat glued to the screen.

"Will you look at him," Dad suddenly commented, "He shouldn't have been in there at all! I don't know why he thought that was a good idea!"

"I don't know how they didn't see that beforehand!" Uncle Jim added.

"You'd have thought it would be obvious to everyone," Evelyn said but was quietened by a glare from her husband.

No one was allowed to talk again.

Finally, there was an ad break and Evelyn started talking. She was telling Dad about Imelda May. "And I don't know what she was thinking," Evelyn told him, "She tottered over the wooden planks they had put out for her and then she sank right into the - "

"Ssshhh!"

The news was back on and Evelyn twittered like a scolded child before sitting down again and being quiet. After the news, Evelyn brought out more food.

"Jim's dinner," she explained, putting more bread and cheese out on the table for everyone else.

"We really don't need anything else, Evelyn," Mum said, "Let Jim have his dinner but we've already eaten. We really couldn't eat anymore."

Evelyn looked taken aback. "Okay, well," she said, "I suppose you were at the Communion. Was there a good spread put on?"

"I'll eat," Dad said, looking at Mum disapprovingly.

Christina sighed loudly. She knew that they were staying for another long while.

"Christina," Uncle Jim said, looking over her head at the TV that was still playing silently in the background, "Is that that lesbian there on the telly?" Christina turned around and looked at the two presenters on the screen. She didn't recognise either of them, but she knew that wasn't the point. She turned back to look at her uncle who had a smirk on his face. Christina's face reddened but no one else noticed.

After Dad had eaten and drank, he suddenly stood up, "Right, we're going!" he said.

Mum was cut short mid-sentence and everyone got up to leave.

Delivering the News

"Luke?" He had a smile on his face when I opened the door, but it didn't make it all the way to his eyes. His black t-shirt had a picture of a monkey on it, swinging upside-down. It wasn't one I recognised, but that wasn't too unusual considering it had been months since I had seen him. His hair was shorter than the last time we had met. It was shorter than I liked it, but it suited his clean-shaven face.

"Jess," his blue eyes sparkled when he spoke.

"What are you doing here?" I was surprised to see him standing there on my front porch. It couldn't be good news.

"I've been calling you, but your phone is off."

"Oh, yeah, it died and I'm waiting for the new one to arrive. Is everything okay?"

"Can I come in?" He was avoiding the question. I had always been able to read him and that hadn't changed apparently. I stood back to let him into the dark, narrow hallway. He was tall. A lot taller than me and he seemed to fill up the whole space.

"In here?" He indicated the door opening into the kitchen/sitting room.

I nodded and followed him. "What's going on?" I asked.

He sat down on the uncomfortable, blue sofa and looked up at me.

"You're freaking me out, Luke. What's going on?"

"It's Peter," he finally said. I waited for him to continue, barely breathing. Not knowing what I could feel. What I wanted to feel. "He passed away," he finally said.

My stomach dropped, that uncomfortable, familiar, dropping feeling that I knew so well from childhood. I stared at him.

"What?" I finally said.

"Your dad. He died. Yesterday." My mouth opened and closed without any sound coming out. "He had a heart attack," Luke continued. "Mum called me. She wanted me to tell you. She wanted to make sure you knew."

He paused. "She didn't want you to be alone when you found out." Another pause. "She - we didn't know if you would find out, or how you'd be told."

I didn't move. I didn't say anything. I stared blankly ahead.

I knew well what Violet, Luke's mum, had meant. She didn't know if anyone in my family would call me to tell me my father had died. She didn't know if I would ever find out. I had imagined this day so many times. I had imagined what it would be like, how it would happen, how I would feel, but now…

I had always known it would be a heart attack. Something quick and instant, that would be how Peter would go. He probably had the heart attack while visiting clients, or checking out a new building he was going to buy and convert into a sixteen-bedroom house to rent out to the highest bidder.

'Find a job you love and you will never work a day in your life' was Peter's mantra. That was his favourite thing to say and work was the only thing he would talk about. The only thing he cared about. That and how he could exploit his children to enhance his work.

Even after the 2008 receivership fiasco, where he had lost the business and properties he had owned, he still jumped straight back on the horse. He spent a few weeks in bed, leaving his wife and children to clean up his mess and he was then straight back at it. But this time, he was using his children's names and details to buy the properties.

During those early recession days, we were all at home trying to help, to do anything because this awful thing had happened and our parents were in their sixties. What would they do, where would they live? Little did we know, they were going to do exactly what they had been doing before the loss and nothing really changed, except that we were now involved, unbeknown to us.

'Find a job you love and you will never work a day in your life' was Peter's mantra. But what that really meant was that he would forsake everything that wasn't work and didn't make him a profit, including his children. Although no one would have believed it, this saint of a father who brought his children to school every morning.

"How wonderful," they said.

"He's so great, he brings them all down every morning in his shorts and sandals, no matter the weather."

I remember so clearly walking on Merrion Road. We were almost at the green post box. "Hurry up!" Dad barked at me, "Stop walking so slowly!" I walked a little faster and he then turned around and grabbed my ponytail, dragging me along.

"Aaahh!" I shouted, in shock more than pain.

"Hurry up!" he growled again, letting me go. I did hurry. I hurried along behind everyone, rubbing my sore head and trying not to cry.

That was the reality of dear old Saint Peter.

"Jess?"

I blinked. Luke was standing now. I looked at him, "Do you want tea?" He looked confused and then nodded. I went over to the kitchenette and picked up the kettle. Turning my back on Luke, I turned on the cold tap and watched the water rush out. I took a deep breath and let it out slowly through my mouth.

"Jess?" I could sense Luke's gaze on me. I shot him a smile over my shoulder before filling the kettle and putting it in its cradle. "I'm sorry that's my news," Luke said as I flicked on the switch.

"It's not your fault. But thank you for telling me." I paused. "Tell your mum I said thanks, too."

"I will. She actually said that if you are looking for somewhere to stay for the funeral, you're always welcome at their house." He paused. "If you want. It's just an option."

I nodded slowly. "Do you think she'd think I was a bad person if I didn't go to the funeral?" I finally asked.

He shook his head. "I don't think she knew if you would or not, she just wanted to offer and for you to know that you can if you want to."

Luke had been the one to tell me that things weren't okay at home. He was sitting on Emily's bed. I was on mine. I was fifteen and he was seventeen. He was jittery and jumpy, and any time there was a sound outside the room he would stop and look at the door. I knew he had something big to tell me because he had been in my room hundreds of times, but never acting like this.

"Will you just spit it out," I finally said.

"I - well. I don't know how to say this." He looked at the ground.

"Luke, I have a history essay to finish. I don't have time to sit here waiting for you to get your shit together. Mr Dunne is going to kill me if I hand in another one late."

"I know. I know," he wiped his sweaty palms on his school trousers and took a deep breath, "I've been thinking this for a while Jess. This," he gestured around the room, "It's not right. How they talk to you. Emily, getting to take up the whole room and you have to do your homework on your bed. She gets a desk and you can't touch it."

"She has exams," I said confused.

"She has a whole college library to study in, and you have exams too. And the way they just cut you off and never listen to you. You don't ever get to pick the film to watch and what you told me your cousins said and did to you last time you visited them! And you had to apologise to them! And Peter just left you there? You said that no one wanted to stay but he just disappeared off with the car so you were stuck there with people who make fun of you? It's not right. It shouldn't happen like that."

What was he talking about?

"And Emily's friend coming into the house and laughing at you for dating someone years ago. Why did her friend even know? It was seven years ago, and what was it to do with him? Who gave him the right to come in here and laugh at you like that, and Emily and your mum joining in?"

"You don't know that. You weren't here," I said defensively.

"And I'm sorry I wasn't. I'd have knocked him out for talking to you like that, and that your mum and Emily just let him. It's not right. Someone should have stopped him. Your mum should have stopped him."

What was going on? How could Luke say these things about my mum? My mum loved Luke. I thought he loved her. What was happening? My parents did their best. Dad worked all the time because he had to. He had to work hard so that we could have clothes and go to good schools. There wasn't anything wrong with that and Mum treated me just like the others. We all had birthday parties and we got presents at Christmas. And she worked too! She didn't have loads of free time to spend with me, so what? It's not like his mum was all over him all the time.

I felt the anger rise up inside me. "Get out," I said suddenly standing up.

"What? No," he was shocked, "Jess, I'm sorry. But you have to know that it's not right."

"Out," I said again coldly., "How dare you sit here saying all of those things! Saying there's something wrong with us! How would you know? Get out!"

"I'm sorry Jess." He was standing now.

"And stop calling me that. My name is Jessica. Only my friends get to call me Jess." He looked crushed. "Get out, and don't come back!"

He stared at me. Neither of us moved. I just wanted him to leave but I wasn't going to say it again. I wasn't going to push him out the door, he knew I wanted him to leave and I wanted him to do it of his own accord. He finally moved towards the door. He opened it and took one look back at me before walking out.

What the hell was that about? I thought. The rage was coursing through me. What had he meant, it wasn't right? Emily needed the extra space. She had big college exams; I was only in third year. My exams didn't matter, they didn't count for anything, but hers did. Of course she needed the desk. I was so shocked that Luke would say such things about my mum. I had never heard him say a bad thing about anyone in my family and now suddenly, here he was lashing into all of them. Even my cousins who he had never met before.

I hated him!

I WAS LYING on my bed the next day, doing my history essay when Mum came into the room. I looked up when she sat down beside me. Something was wrong. I knew something was wrong. I could read her like a book. I sat up.

Tears started running down her cheeks. I stared at her. Oh God, what was it?

"It's Alex Murphy," she finally said, "Luke's dad," She started crying again, "He died."

That couldn't be true. I had only just seen Alex that morning. He was getting into the car as I was leaving for school. I had been afraid to look over at the house for fear that I would see Luke. Alex had waved at me and smiled. I smiled back and walked on quickly.

"That's not true," I finally said. Mum put her head in her hands and cried properly in response. I sat back against the wall and stared at her. It couldn't be true. No way. I had only just seen him. People didn't just die like that.

After a few minutes, Mum wiped her tears away and composed herself. "I just thought you should know," she said, "With you and Luke being so friendly."

I nodded. She put her hand on my knee. "Are you okay?"

"Eh," was all I could say. I finally nodded and Mum got up to leave the room. I didn't move. Poor Luke, was all I could think. Poor Luke, and Eloise, and Ben. Oh God. But it couldn't be true. I got up and went out to the kitchen. Emily and Mum were there. They were talking in hushed voices and stopped when I came in.

"Have you talked to Luke?" Emily asked, turning to me.

"Are you sure it's true? I just saw him this morning,"

"I know," Emily said, "So did I. It's so sad."

No one said anything else. My question went unanswered. I went back to my room and sat on the bed. My history homework sat looking at me, but all I could think about was the last thing I had said to Luke. How awful I had been to him.

I didn't know what to do. Should I call? Should I go over? Would he want to see me? Would he ever speak to me again? I had been so mean.

I couldn't believe this had happened. That his dad died the day after I kicked him out of the house. I couldn't remember ever fighting with Luke, and this was when I chose to do it? God, I was so awful! How could I have been so mean to him? But it was his fault. I suddenly remembered. All of those awful things he had said about my family, they didn't deserve that. They had been nothing but kind to him. How could he?

I spent most of that night going over in my head between being so sad and feeling awful for them, and then feeling awful for how I had spoken to him, and terrible for what he had said. I was exhausted by the time morning came. I went to school the next day because I didn't know what else to do, but as soon as I walked in the door, I knew it had been a bad idea.

"Oh my God, Jess, I can't believe it!" Mary McCarthy said coming up to me at the front door, "My mum told me. It's so awful! How are they all?" I looked at her blankly. Mary McCarthy had never spoken to me before. We had been in the same year in school since we were twelve but this was the most she had ever said to me. I walked off without responding to her.

"Is it really true?" Noelle Williams at least waited until I had taken off my coat and put it in my locker to approach me. I knew Noelle more than I knew Mary, but I still didn't have much interest in talking to her.

"He fell off a ladder," I heard Micheál Ó Máille saying in maths.

By lunchtime, Eloise and Ben's friends had found me and asked how they were. I told them they were baring up as well as anyone could in a situation like this.

A lie. I had no idea how they were. How would I know if they were baring up when I hadn't gone near the house? I had glanced over quickly as I left for school that morning, but I didn't dare to go near it. The previous night's mental gymnastics had left me feeling more and more awful for the way I had spoken to Luke. The way we had left things. I couldn't stop thinking about how terrible it would have been if he had been the one to die.

"Are you coming over to the house?" I blinked. Mum was looking at me from the sitting room door. I had the TV on but I had no idea what was playing. I remembered turning it on when I came in from school, but I must have just stared blankly at it ever since.

"Okay." It seemed like the only appropriate answer. I stood up and followed her out to the hall. She was carrying a large casserole dish that was covered with tinfoil.

The front door of the Murphy's house was open and there were a few people arriving with us. Everyone looked sombre and greeted each other with small nods. The house felt different, unsettling. I usually felt lighter when I walked in this front door, today I felt sick with sadness and anxiety. The atmosphere was heavy and the energy from everyone else felt almost oppressive. Violet was standing by the wall behind the sofa when we entered. Mum went over to her and shook her hand. I stood and watched, too afraid to go closer.

"Jess," Violet smiled at me warmly. I had always loved Luke's mum. She had always included me at dinner time without asking, and she never seemed to get annoyed when I was there all the time. Now, she pulled me in for a hug and we stood like that for a long time. "Thank you for coming," she finally said when we broke away, her eyes glistening with tears. I gave her a small smile and then turned away as Mum started talking to her.

I recognised a few people in the room but most of them were strangers. Then I saw little Eloise. She was sitting on the arm of a chair talking to an older woman I didn't recognise, with a forced smile on her face. She was ten years old, but in that moment, she looked much older. I suppose the death of a parent probably does that to you. Ben, who was four years older than Eloise, and four younger than Luke, was standing by a table laden with food. He was absentmindedly picking at a plate of sandwiches. In contrast, Ben looked much younger than his fourteen years. He looked like a lost little boy. I couldn't see Luke. I went out to the hall but he wasn't there either, neither was he in the kitchen.

"He's in his room." It was Eloise. She was standing by the kitchen door when I turned around. I hadn't noticed how tired she looked when I had seen her before.

"Why?"

She shrugged. "He hasn't come out much."

I nodded and then said, "I'm sorry for your loss."

She gave me a small smile.

"Do you think I should go up?" I asked, glancing towards the stairs.

"Yes," She looked surprised that I even asked. Luke had obviously not told her what I had said. I walked slowly towards the stairs, pushing past the neighbours that crowded the narrow hallway. Hung on the walls, on the way up, were photos of happier times, photos from family holidays, photos from the back garden and family occasions. I even featured in a few, but now all I could see was how happy Alex looked, how happy everyone looked. I wondered if we would ever feel that happy again.

I stood awkwardly at the top of the stairs for a minute before taking a deep breath and walking up to the familiar blue door. I shifted from foot to foot before I knocked lightly. There was no answer. What if he didn't want to see me? I thought, what if he's too angry with me?

I knocked again. "Luke?" I finally said, "Are you in there?"

"Jess?" I heard movement inside the room. The door opened and a tired, sad Luke looked out at me. He looked like he hadn't showered in days. He was wearing a crumpled grey t-shirt and navy tracksuit bottoms that had seen better days. His hair was sticking up in all the wrong places and he looked exhausted. "What are you doing here?"

"Your Dad died."

"Yeah." He looked dejected. He paused and then looked at me again. "You were so angry."

"I know, I'm sorry. I shouldn't have kicked you out."

"No, I'm sorry. I shouldn't have said anything. I was wrong. I'm really sorry."

"I didn't know if I should come over."

"I didn't think you would."

We looked at each other for a minute and then laughed. It was a deep belly laugh, a laugh that was much bigger than it needed to be, but it felt so good. It felt right. It felt normal.

"You need to have a shower," I said when we finally stopped laughing, "You need to shower and dress in something that's not," I looked with disdain at his outfit, "Not that and you need to go down and help your mum cater to all of these people."

I SMILED AT THE MEMORY. Luke was looking at me with concern again.

"I was thinking about us laughing outside your room while everyone was downstairs mourning your dad's passing. I'm sure they thought we were manic."

Luke smiled now. "We probably were," he said, "I hadn't slept at all since you kicked me out of the house and then the news came about Dad and I just collapsed. I didn't know what to do. I thought I had lost my best friend and my dad in less than 24 hours."

"It was awful. I remember not wanting to ever fight with you again for fear that something terrible would happen to someone."

"I don't know how I would have gotten through those next few months without you," he said.

I smiled remembering. "I just moved into your house. I thought I was helping."

Luke looked surprised, "You were! I really don't know what any of us would have done without you!"

"Really?"

"Did you not know that?"

"I -" I stopped and then I remembered. "I was doing something good."

"Of course you were. We absolutely needed you. *I* needed you. Why would you think you weren't doing something good?"

I hadn't told Luke. I hadn't told anyone. I didn't know where to start, "I think Emily must have found out from Eloise that I was sleeping in your bed and she told Mum and Dad and they - they had a go at me, because they presumed we were having sex."

Luke's eyes widened with shock.

"They lost it," I continued, "They were so disappointed in me. They called me into the room and told me that I was spending too much time in your house. They said I was giving a family, that didn't care about me, all of my time and they weren't appreciating it. They said you were using me. I believed them. I felt awful and stupid, that I had fallen for it, that you were all using me. And then Mum said that I was giving myself to a boy who didn't care about me like that, he couldn't care because he was too young. I was going to regret it and Dad said I would ruin my life properly with a baby if I continued to whore myself out. He said that I would be known as the village bicycle and no one would want me after that. It took me a few minutes to even know what they were implying because it was so far from what we ever would have thought about!"

Luke was now red with anger. I could see he was about to explode. His mouth opened and closed but no sound came out. I stood looking at the floor. It turned out the shame lived even if the words were spoken out loud, too.

"You really believed them?" Luke's voice finally returned.

I nodded. "I've literally only just realised that it was all bullshit," I said, "I remember that I didn't go back to your house for a week or so after that and you didn't seem to notice."

"Didn't notice? I fell apart. I was devastated. I couldn't sleep without you with me for at least two weeks. But I thought you had had to go home. We'd taken up so much of your time," he paused, "I cannot believe that bastard said all of that to you! That's awful, and it proves that everything I had said the night before Dad died was true."

I nodded, "I think everything you said that day was 100% true, I just didn't want to hear it at the time." Neither of us said anything for a while. We stood in silence, each in our own thoughts about what had happened all those years ago. "Well, one thing I will say," I finally said, "I will not be falling apart over the death of my father like you did."

We both laughed.

Epilogue

As these stories are all based on things that happened when I was growing up, you can imagine the trauma and the abuse I suffered.

I was bullied by the very people who were supposed to protect me. I never had a safe place to go, a safe place to turn. I found solace in books. I loved reading fiction books and I then took those stories into my head and I created whole new worlds for myself there. I spent most of my childhood inside my own head because it was a nicer place to be than the real world.

For as long as I can remember, I have felt like there was an evilness, a poison in my life. I didn't know what it was or what to do about it. It was just there and it felt like a permanent fixture. I soon started to feel like that evilness, that poison, was me. It was in me and I was evil and poisonous.

Two years ago, I went through what I describe in *She's Forgotten Me* and the peace and calm I experienced then allowed me to imagine a life without my biological family. It allowed me to feel what it would be like if I didn't have contact with them, and the peace made it all feel possible. So I slowly extracted myself from the relationship with my mother. My mother was the only member of my biological family that made an effort to contact me. But just like Jess's mother does in that story, my mother slowly stopped contacting me when my visits home became less frequent. Once I'd decided I didn't want a relationship with her, she came at me full force. I got weekly, sometimes more frequent messages asking me to meet her, and when I asked for space, it wasn't granted, so I resorted to blocking. Now, my entire family is blocked. I have no contact with anyone I grew up with, and my life has come on in leaps and bounds.

No contact with them allowed me to get to know myself. It allowed me to rediscover parts of myself that my family wouldn't allow me to show and discover other parts of me that I never knew existed. My family had kept me in such a tiny, tight space that I couldn't do anything I wanted to do. They wanted me to look and be a certain way that I am not, I was not and I will never be.

Extracting myself from my biological family was one of the best decisions I have ever made, but it has not come without its challenges. Challenges that I would happily go through again ten times over to get to where I am now.

It took a huge amount of courage, a lot of tears, years of meditation, lots of therapy and an incredible support system around me, as well as a huge faith in myself to get me to where I am now, but it has been so incredibly worth it.

That evilness and poison has now gone. When I stopped contact with my family that poison seemed to just disappear. It turns out there was nothing evil or poisonous about me, or in me, all along. I was not the problem.

If my stories resonate for you, I am sending you so much love. It is tough, but you are not alone and you can do this. Whatever this looks like for you, you can do it!

RESOURCES

Find a therapist that works with emotional and parental abuse. I cannot overstate how much therapy helped me.

More information
Podcast: Insight:
Exposing Narcissism

Book: *You are not the Problem: The Impact of Narcissism and Emotional Abuse and How to Heal* by Helen Villiers and Katie McKenna

Find a therapist that works with emotional and parental abuse. I cannot overstate how much therapy helped me.

GET HELP...

Here are some charities where help can be found:
<u>Women's Aid</u>
Mens Aid
Samaritans

If you are concerned for a child's welfare:
<u>Barnado's</u>
Tulsa

Printed in Great Britain
by Amazon